THE LITTLE PRAIRIE BOOK OF BERRIES

Recipes for Saskatoons, Sea Buckthorn,
Haskap Berries and More

SHERYL NORMANDEAU

ILLUSTRATIONS BY TREE ABRAHAM & MERYL HULSE

TOUCHWOOD

Contents

Introduction

Do you have a chokecherry tree in your front yard or did you just plant a haskap shrub? What about those currants and sour cherries* you saw at the U-pick farm last year, or the saskatoon berries you harvested from the wild? Or sea buckthorn, that thorny plant with the orange berries, that you found at the nursery and are keen to try in your own yard? Are you interested in doing something with the fruit these plants produce? Of course you are! Not only is it a chance to try fresh flavours and new dishes, but you'll be using the bounty of the plants you grow (or forage from). As added benefits, using garden- or wild-grown produce is economical, and you'll be reducing food waste.

Chokecherries, haskap berries, saskatoons, currants, sour cherries, and sea buckthorn berries are all gaining popularity in prairie (and Canadian) gardens—and some of these plants may be found in the wild, as well. For many of these fruits, however, it is difficult to find a lot of practical, tasty, and simple recipes to use them in, especially for home cooks with tight budgets and busy schedules. *The Little Prairie Book of Berries* is filled with these sorts of recipes, including meat, poultry, and fish dishes; vegetable and grain dishes; desserts and baked goods; beverages; and preserved foods. (And if you have specific dietary requirements, there are substitutions for ingredients to conveniently create gluten-free, nut-free, vegetarian, vegan, and dairy-free alternatives wherever possible.) I want to inspire cooks and gardeners to stop thinking of these fruits as "exotic" and unfamiliar and start reaping the delicious rewards found in our own backyards. Alongside the recipes, I also give you some tips to help plant, cultivate, and maintain these small fruit shrubs and trees in your garden, so that you can keep benefiting from bountiful harvests for years to come.

Let's get growing and eating!

---

*Sour cherries may have a round fruit reminiscent of a berry, but botanically, they are actually a drupe (stone fruit). Despite their official non-berry status, I've included them in *The Little Prairie Book of Berries* because there just doesn't seem to be a lot of creative and delicious sour cherry recipes out there. That stops now!

Important Things to Know
While Using This Book

INGREDIENT SUBSTITUTIONS

Substitutions may be made in certain recipes to accommodate dietary restrictions, allergies, or preferences.

Gluten-free flour blends may be swapped cup-for-cup for all-purpose flour. I have tested all of the recipes in the book using gluten-free substitutes, and there are only two recipes where gluten-free flour is not recommended: Haskap Berry and White Chocolate Scones (page 32) and Chokecherry Pudding Cake (page 89). The gluten in the flour is essential to the successful creation of these recipes. I also would advise not using single-ingredient gluten free flours such as almond or coconut in any of the recipes (unless I've called for them), as they can create problems. Coconut flour, for example, will soak up every drop of liquid in a recipe, and the whole thing will come out dry and crumbly unless you alter the amount of wet ingredients.

Nut or seed milks may be substituted for dairy milk. Coconut milk is another option, but bear in mind that its strong, unique flavour may not be exactly right for recipes in this book.

Vegan cheeses and meat substitutes or tofu may take the place of most dairy and meat ingredients.

There are dairy-free, vegan substitutes for butter available at most grocery stores and markets. Coconut oil is another alternative that can be used in place of butter, but again, it may alter the flavour of a given recipe.

Other ingredients, such as nuts, may be omitted in most recipes. There are exceptions. For example, peanuts are one of the key ingredients in Haskap Berry Peanut Energy Bites on page 33 and Sour Cherry and Peanut Butter Bars, found on page 167, and the recipes will fail without them or another nut substitute.

HOW TO MAKE A FLAX OR CHIA "EGG"

If you can't eat eggs, and the recipe calls for one or two, you can make an easy egg substitute. To take the place of one egg, combine 1 Tbsp ground flaxseed and 2 Tbsp water in a cup. (If you don't have flaxseed on hand, you can mix 1 Tbsp chia seeds with 2½ Tbsp water.) Let the mixture sit for 5 minutes, then use it in the recipe. Don't use this substitute if the recipe calls for three or more eggs, as it may not bind or thicken ingredients, the way that eggs will.

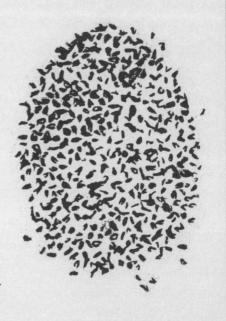

A Note About Substituting Berries and Using Fresh or Frozen Ingredients in Recipes

Where applicable, I've mentioned at the beginning of each recipe if a berry or fruit may be substituted for another. In these cases, use the same measurements given in the recipe.

Sometimes it's best to use fresh berries—in a trifle, for example. Other times, you'll want to use frozen because if you use fresh, the volume of juice will cause your baked product to lose a little in the appearance department. Many times it doesn't matter which one you choose. I have marked recipes where it is essential to use either fresh or frozen berries. If there is no indication in the recipe, feel free to use either fresh or frozen berries.

DIETARY CONSIDERATIONS

I have included an at-a-glance legend for each recipe listing dietary considerations. Recipes may be:

GF	GLUTEN FREE
DF	DAIRY FREE
NF	NUT FREE
V	VEGETARIAN
VG	VEGAN

FORAGING FOR WILD BERRIES

A few of the berries in this book—chokecherries, black currants, and saskatoons—grow wild in many regions of the prairies. If you wish to forage for berries instead of cultivating and harvesting them from your garden plants, the Gardener's Path website recommends several guidelines to do it safely and respectfully.

1. Be absolutely certain you can identify the plants you are harvesting from. Don't guess! Eating the wrong berries can have potentially deadly consequences. If you don't know, don't pick. There are many excellent regional plant identification books available to use as reference material; add one or more into your backpack. Examine all of the parts of the plant to ensure it matches the given descriptions. Learn something about the types of ecosystems where these plants are likely to grow, which can aid in proper identification. If the plant you are seeing in a densely forested area typically grows in an arid grassland, it may not match the ID you are thinking of. Another thing to think about is the timing of the harvest. If you know that chokecherries are not typically ripe until August, and you find a dark berry ready in June, likely it's not a chokecherry.

2. Do not trespass onto private property. Always ask for permission if you want to pick berries on private land. Do not pick berries on protected land, including nature preserves and parks. These areas may contain rare or endangered plants that should not be disturbed. As well, the act of foraging may disrupt the activities of wildlife and birds in the area, which may do harm. Don't break the law or endanger plants and animals for a few pieces of fruit!

3. Do not pick every berry from the plant. Leave some for wildlife and birds or for other human foragers.

4. Do not harvest berries from plants that look diseased or that have had pesticides sprayed on them.

5. Wear comfortable clothes so you can move easily in difficult terrain. Long sleeves and pants are essential for protection against hot sun or cool temperatures, to prevent rashes from touching plants, and to ward off insect bites. (And if you live in tick country, exposing bare skin is a terrible idea.) Sturdy boots or hiking shoes are a must.

6. Bring along a first aid kit. Tick kits containing the accoutrements necessary to safely remove the vile little arachnids may be useful as well.

7. Animals such as bears may also be in the mood for a little berry picking at the same time you are, so be vigilant. Watch for signs that they are in the area, and carry bear spray and an air horn for protection. (Confirm regional laws to ensure that you are permitted to possess bear spray.)

8. Don't forage alone. This is safety precaution if one of you gets hurt. If you do go solo, let someone know where you are and what time to anticipate your return.

9. Harvest in the morning instead of during the heat of the day. Have a cooler waiting in the vehicle to transport your berries home.

10. Finally, have fun and enjoy the outdoor experience!

U-PICK FARMS

If you don't have access to berries from your own garden and foraging for wild fruit isn't possible, why not spend a day at a local U-pick farm? Many prairie growers and orchardists open their farms every year for visitors to enjoy. Be sure to plan ahead to obtain the best experience from your U-pick excursion. Not all farms offer the same varieties of berries; some may specialize in just one or two types. Know your harvest times: you won't be able to pick haskap berries in September, for example. Most growers have their own websites and update regularly on social media when it's time to visit the farm. Remember that some farms are not open every day of the week, and they may have limited hours of operation. (Bear in mind, as well, that it's best to pick berries in the early morning or late evening for optimum freshness. Try to time your excursion to accommodate this.) Some U-pick farms may require reservations. I would recommend always phoning ahead before making the drive to the site.

While you're at the U-pick, be sure to follow the rules set out by the farmer. Most of them live onsite and you are a guest on their property. Some farms will not permit you to bring your pets to the farm, or they will require you to keep your dogs on a leash. While outside food and picnicking is allowed at some farms, others do not permit it. Ask before you head out to prevent any misunderstandings.

Be prepared for the weather (I have gone out in mid-June while wet snow was falling and more than a few times faced withering heat in July and August). Insect bites, and scrapes and rashes from prickly plants are common occurrences, so cover up accordingly and pack a small first aid kit. Don't forget to bring bottled water to drink; while some U-picks offer concession, most don't. Depending on what you are planning to pick, a folding camp chair will make the task more comfortable. One saskatoon U-pick I frequent lends custom-made one-legged wooden stools to its customers to use while picking from the low shrubs.

Some growers will charge a small grazing fee in addition to the cost of the berries you pick, which will be payable when you arrive. And if you want to forgo the actual picking and just purchase the berries, some U-pick operations will have pre-picked pails ready for you for a small extra charge.

EATING FRESH BERRIES

Due to their huge pits and their extremely sour taste, it is not recommended to eat chokecherries fresh off the tree. You'll want to process them before eating. Sea buckthorn berries have several hard, crunchy seeds in them, and they are tart in flavour—not to everyone's liking—but they may still be eaten fresh. Saskatoons, haskap berries, and currants are all suitable for eating out of hand (although some people find haskap berries and currants a bit too sour for their palates). Sour cherries are delicious—if a bit tart—when eaten fresh, but remember that they have a big stone inside of them that must not be eaten.

If you plan to use fresh berries in a recipe, make sure you get the just-harvested fruit into the refrigerator as soon as you can after picking it to prevent it from degrading in quality and flavour. Ideally, use fresh berries up within two days of picking. (Some, such as saskatoons, currants, and haskap cultivars with firm skins, may hold up nicely for up to one week.) If you cannot use up all of the fresh fruit right away, you can freeze it using several different methods.

PROCESSING AND STORING BERRIES

Open freezing berries

If you want to freeze berries without sugar and don't want them to clump up in storage, try this method: Get a large baking sheet and line it with a piece of parchment paper. Wash the berries well, and pick out any stems and other debris (including insects!). Spread the berries in a single layer on the parchment paper, and pop the baking sheet, uncovered, into a large freezer for at least six hours. Remove the baking sheet and immediately pack the berries into plastic freezer bags. Label the bags and put them back into the freezer until ready to use. Using this method, the berries freeze individually, which makes them easier to work with. Just measure out the amount you want when using them in baking and cooking.

Open frozen berries should be used within six months.

Freezing berries with the dry sugar pack method

You can freeze whole saskatoons, haskap berries, currants, sour cherries, and sea buckthorn berries with the dry sugar pack method or you can purée them. The book *Storing Home Grown Fruit or Veg* by Caroline Radula-Scott suggests adding 1 cup of granulated sugar per 4 cups of fruit and stirring to combine. Pack the sugar-packed berries into freezer-safe containers and label them. Use the berries up within one year. (Sugar-packed fruit lasts longer in storage than open frozen fruit does.) You can use sugar-packed berries in fruit smoothies, fruit cobblers and crisps, and, combined with a thickener such as cornstarch, for pie filling.

Drying berries

While you can dry berries in a low temperature oven, it can take a very long time to remove enough moisture to prevent spoiling during storage. Using a dehydrator is a faster, more energy-efficient option. Remember, the time it takes to dehydrate the berries will depend on the ripeness of the fruit, as well as how many you can cram into the dehydrator trays. (They will dry more quickly if there is more air circulation in the machine.)

For sour cherries, set your dehydrator to 135°F. Pit and cut the cherries in half, then set them in the dehydrator tray with the skin sides down. Dehydrate them for 22 to 26 hours.

There is a bit of preparation involved before you can dehydrate saskatoons, currants, haskap berries, and sea buckthorn berries. (I'm not mentioning chokecherries because you'd have to pit all of those tiny berries, and that's just a messy job no one wants to undertake. I would recommend juicing them instead.) Saskatoons and currants should be blanched before you dehydrate them. This helps break their skins to facilitate faster drying. Sea buckthorn berries and haskap berries are a bit too fragile to blanch; just dehydrate them as is.

To blanch the berries, fill a large saucepan with water. Bring the water to a rolling boil.

Place the berries in a heat-safe colander with a handle. Dip the berries into the boiling water, making sure they are completely covered with the water. Let them sit in the water for 1 minute, then remove them from the heat.

Immediately plunge the berries into a bowl of ice water. Allow them to cool completely, then spread them out on a board and pat them dry with paper towels.

The berries are now ready to dehydrate. The dehydrator should be set to 135°F. The berries will take between 14 and 18 hours to dehydrate.

Completely cool the dehydrated berries before packing them into a dry, airtight container. Store them in a cool, dry place for up to 1 year. (Check the berries periodically to ensure they haven't gone bad in storage.)

If you want to dehydrate berries using your oven, set the temperature to 140°F. Blanch the berries, and set them on a baking sheet that has been covered with a piece of parchment paper. Place them in the oven. Check on their progress at the 10-hour mark, and keep checking periodically thereafter.

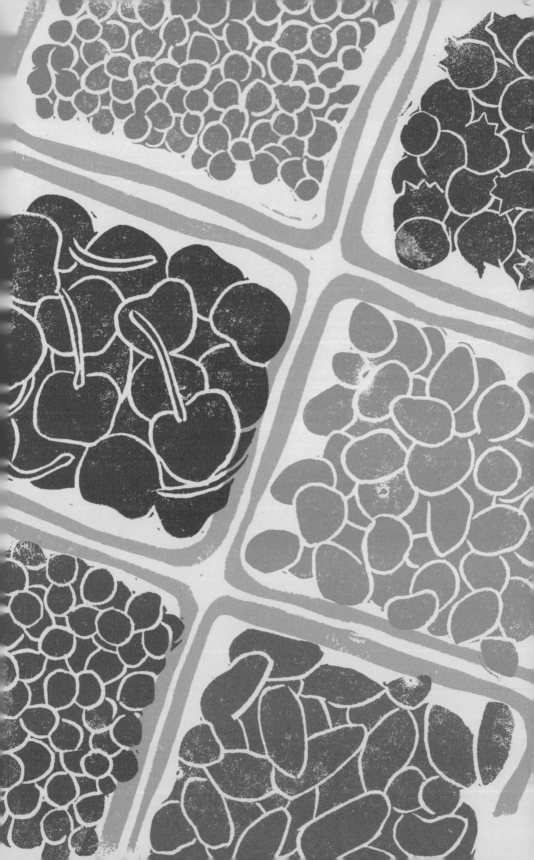

How to make fruit leather

Haskap berry fruit leather is one of my favourite things to take along on a hike. Sour cherries, saskatoons, and currants make great fruit leather as well.

> 2 cups berries, chopped
> 1 cup water
> 1 Tbsp honey
> 1 tsp lemon juice
> ½ tsp vegetable oil, for greasing the pan

Combine the berries and water in a medium saucepan. Over high heat, bring the berries to a boil, then reduce the heat to medium. Simmer the berries until they are soft, 10 to 15 minutes.

Remove the berries from the heat, and allow them to cool to room temperature. Add the honey and lemon juice. Using an immersion or a stand blender, purée the mixture.

Rub the fruit leather tray of the dehydrator with the vegetable oil. Evenly spread the fruit purée into the fruit leather tray. The layer should be about ¼-inch thick.

Dry the fruit leather at 135°F for 4 hours. Check it at that point; if it still has a liquid consistency, dry it for longer. Finished fruit leather should be a bit tacky, not completely crispy, when dry. (You should be able to roll it up!)

You can also dry the berry purée in a 140°F oven. Place a piece of parchment paper on a baking sheet. Spread the purée in a ¼-inch layer over the parchment. Dry it in the oven for 5 hours. Check the consistency of the fruit leather at that stage, and dry it for longer, if necessary.

Completely cool the fruit leather before storing. Cut it into strips using a pair of kitchen scissors. Store the fruit leather for up to 1 month at room temperature (but check it periodically to ensure that it hasn't grown any mould).

How to make berry juice

Many of the recipes in this book call for berry juice, rather than the whole fruit. If you have the budget, the space, and the desire to purchase a steam juicer for any of your cooking and baking projects, using this marvelous device to extract juice is easy. If you don't have a steam juicer (like me!), just follow these easy steps:

1. Place the required quantity of berries in a large saucepan and cover them with water. Bring the berries to a boil over high heat. Turn the heat down and allow the berries to simmer for 10 minutes. Remove the berries from the heat and allow them to cool to room temperature.

2. If the berries have not been broken down by the cooking process, you can help them along. Use a potato masher or—better yet—an immersion blender to crush them.

3. Strain the berries into a bowl through a piece of fine cheese-cloth, a fine mesh sieve, or a jelly strainer, if you have one. The resulting juice can then be used in your favourite recipes or frozen for later use.

4. The berry pulp can be composted if it doesn't contain seeds. I prefer to save the pulp from fruits and berries that don't have hard or inedible seeds (for example, saskatoons, haskap berries, and currants) to mix with other fruits such as apples, peaches, or plums in cobblers and crisps or in muffins. Be creative and don't waste the leftovers. Some people enjoy the crunch of sea buck-thorn seeds and will use the leftover pulp from them as well.

SAFE AND PROPER CANNING PROCEDURES
WHEN MAKING JAMS AND JELLIES

There are some jam and jelly recipes in this cookbook, which require processing to make them shelf-stable for long-term storage. Improper canning methods can result in unsafe food, so be sure to follow all sterilization and processing procedures to a T, and use the correct equipment.

A few things to note before you make the jams and jellies in this book:

1. Do not make double or triple batches. If you want larger quantities than the recipe calls for, make the entire recipe more than once. Altering the recipe may result in a failure, and this wastes ingredients, time, and money.

2. Measure accurately—this goes for any recipe.

3. These recipes have not been tested with alternative sweeteners. Sugar helps to set jams and jellies and switching it up with something else may not result in proper gel formation. It may also alter the flavour and possibly compromise the safety of long-term storage.

4. If you plan to store jam or jelly at room temperature, you must process it in a boiling water canner. This is for your safety. Otherwise, eat it all right away or refrigerate it for up to 1 month.

How to make and process jams and jellies

1. Wash your jars, screw bands, and sealing discs in hot, soapy water.

2. Place the number of jars that are required in the recipe in the rack of a boiling water canner. Cover the jars with water and bring the water to a boil over high heat for 10 minutes. Turn the heat down to medium and allow the jars to simmer in the hot water.

3. Place the sealing discs in a shallow bowl filled with hot water. This will help the seals soften.

4. Cook the jam or jelly according to the recipe.

5. Use a jar lifter to remove the empty jars from the canner. Empty the water from the jars back into the canner. Do not turn off the heat on the stovetop.

6. Ladle the hot jam or jelly into the jars, to within ¼-inch below the top of the jar. Make sure there are no drippings on the rims of the jars—if you spot any, wipe them off.

7. Place the hot sealing disc on each jar rim and attach the screw bands. Do not overtighten the screw bands, as that can potentially alter the seal.

8. Return the filled jars to the canner using the jar lifter. The water should be at a level approximately 1 inch above the jars. (If some water has evaporated, add hot water to the canner.) Bring the water back to a boil, and cover the canner.

9. The Better Homes and Gardens website suggests that jams and jellies should be processed for 10 minutes if you live at an altitude of 1,000 feet above sea level or less. If you live at 1,001

to 3,000 feet above sea level, process for 15 minutes. If you live at an altitude of 3,001 to 6,000 feet above sea level, as I do in Calgary, process for 20 minutes.

10. When the processing time is complete, turn the heat off, and remove the lid of the canner. Allow the water to stop simmering, then remove the jars with the jar lifter. Do not tip the jars over. Place the jars upright on a tea towel on the counter, and allow them to cool for 24 hours. Do not touch the screw bands at this point.

11. After the jars have cooled, check to see that they have sealed. The sealing discs will have depressed downward; you may have heard the popping sounds they made when they did this. If the jars are not sealed, you can refrigerate the jam or jelly, and use it up within a few weeks.

12. Remove the screw bands before storing the jams and jellies. Store them in a cool, dark place. To minimize the risk of breakage and possible sealing issues, do not stack the jars on top of each other on the shelf. Eat the contents within 1 year.

How to reach the gel point

Some of the jam and jelly recipes featured in this book do not have any added pectin in them, so you need to cook them until they reach a gel point. That means the jam or jelly has reached a stage where it will set properly and not be runny. There is a method to determine the gel point using a plate and your freezer, but unless you've been making jams and jellies for a long time, it can be difficult to correctly assess the gel point using that particular test. A reliable and easier way is to use a candy thermometer.

Insert the thermometer vertically into the jam or jelly, and do not let the tip of the thermometer touch the bottom of the saucepan. The thermometer should read 220°F if you live at sea level. The National Center for Home Food Preservation recommends that for every 1,000 feet of altitude above sea level, subtract 2°F from that amount. For example, Calgary is situated at 3,438 feet above sea level, so I need my thermometer to read 214°F.

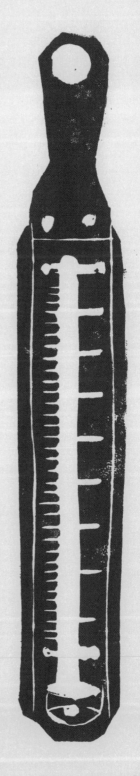

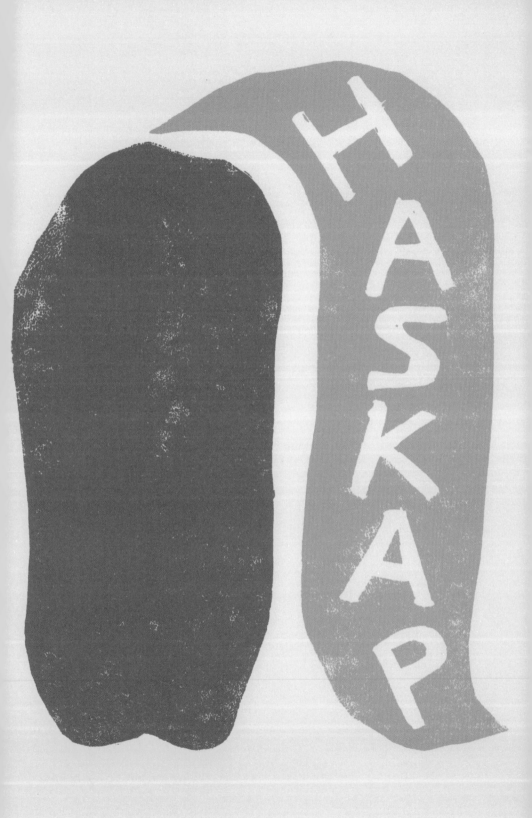

Edible blue honeysuckle seems like a relative newcomer to Canadian prairie gardens and orchards, but it actually has a long history. According to Dr. Bob Bors at the University of Saskatchewan, numerous species and subspecies of *Lonicera caerulea* are native to Europe and North America but in the past have not typically been cultivated for food, as the berries generally tasted poorly (a bit of an understatement, actually!). Early blue honeysuckle breeding in Alberta in the 1950s was a testament to the awful taste of the fruit and was quickly abandoned. In the same decade, Russian plant breeders had more success working with the subspecies *L. edulis* and *L. kamtschatica* to produce a more palatable fruit. A small island in Japan, Hokkaido, has the distinction of cultivating delicious berries from honeysuckle plants, which they began domesticating in the 1980s. They call the blue honeysuckle haskap, a name which is also used by Canadian breeders (mostly since produce was initially intended to be promoted to a Japanese market). Canadian breeders have culled germplasm from both Japanese and Russian sources to use for their haskap breeding program, which was initiated in 1998 at the University of Saskatchewan. A joint breeding program by Oregon State University preceded the U of S program.

Cultivar development is ongoing, with plants being selected for traits such as powdery mildew resistance, high antioxidant content, flavour, size and texture of berries, and ease of mechanical harvest (which is directly related to commercial production).

Hardiness is definitely not a concern with haskap plants: The Russian cultivars may withstand winter temperatures of -58°F and the University of Saskatchewan cultivars are cold hardy to the high -40s (Fahrenheit and Celsius!). Plants are rated to zone 2. These are the ultimate prairie berry!

Haskap is a deciduous shrub with a tidy, rounded habit. Most cultivars reach a height of about 5 feet with a spread of 3.25 feet. Some cultivars are not as upright in shape as others, but I wouldn't characterize them as sprawling or unkempt, and they don't sucker.

The small yellow flowers appear in April through May, depending on geographical location. The blooms may be plain, but they are absolute bee magnets! The leaves are dark green and may be smooth or, less commonly, sport fine hairs. Flowers can tolerate temperatures as low as 19°F, which is important, since the weather is sometimes not very warm on the prairies in April and May. Fruit appears 6 to 8 weeks after flowering, usually in early to mid-June, before most other fruit crops are getting underway. Once the berries appear, it can take up to 7 to 10 days for them to ripen fully. Some newer cultivars have been bred to bloom later in the season, which may minimize the risk of frost damage in late spring (as well as increase the potential for pollination).

As haskap flowers are self-incompatible (they cannot be fertilized by their own pollen), a helping hand in the way of a suitable, unrelated pollinizer is required in order for plants to set fruit. The pollinizer plant must bloom at close to the same time as the cultivar it is pollinating. Haskap plants must have specific pollinizer cultivars for fruit production to be successful—not every plant is compatible with another. Fortunately, one pollinizer plant will typically pollinate five to eight haskap plants, which helps if you want to produce a lot of fruit. Both the crop and the pollinizers should be planted as close to each other as possible so that bees can easily reach them. If you don't want to go to the trouble of matching up compatible cultivars, you can purchase properly matched "male" and "female" plants at some garden centres (this is a misnomer as individual haskap berry plants are not specifically male or female and you don't need a male and a female plant to produce fruit, but the marketing strategy does make things easier for the consumer).

GROWING HASKAP BERRIES

Haskap is adaptable to a wide range of soil textures, including clay, but it prefers loam rich in organic matter. Unless your soil is already nice and fertile, a light side-dressing of compost in the spring is a good idea. Ensure your soil has good drainage. Haskap can tolerate wet soils, but it will not thrive in them.

Planting new haskap plants should be done in late spring or early summer, before the weather becomes too hot. If heat is an issue, young plants may be sheltered by row cover fabric. Haskap does not require staking at any stage of growth. Space individual plants 3.25 feet apart.

Cover the shrubs with bird netting to protect the harvest—birds positively *adore* the berries! Lift the netting away from the plants using stakes, and peg it down with landscape staples. Use netting with very fine mesh to prevent birds from becoming tangled in it. Haskap doesn't seem to be bothered by many other pests. Diseases are seldom found in haskap plants either. Powdery mildew does not affect the fruit, as it usually sets in during the hot, humid days of mid-summer after the plants have already fruited, but foliage can definitely become infected. Maintaining sufficient air circulation through pruning may discourage mildew.

Haskap requires regular, deep watering, especially during the first few years as shrubs establish themselves. Shallow irrigation only promotes weak rooting and should not be encouraged. Soil texture will influence watering: If the soil is sandy and drains readily, it will be necessary to water more often than if the soil is composed of heavy clay and does not allow water to flow freely through it. Both watering and fertilizer application should be discontinued in late autumn to permit the shrubs to enter a state of winter dormancy.

It is necessary to pull all the weeds that grow between haskap shrubs, as the weeds will take up essential nutrients and water that should be made available to the haskap plants.

Prune in late winter or early spring before plants begin to bud out. Dead wood should be removed, and shrubs may be thinned to promote better air circulation (which will aid in the fight against powdery mildew). No more than 25 percent of the wood should be pruned out at a time. As the shrubs age, thick stems will require removal in order to ensure that plants remain easy to harvest.

NOW FOR THE GOOD STUFF: WHEN CAN I PICK FRUIT?

Most haskap cultivars will begin producing some fruit in their second year, with peak yield at five years. Individual plants produce approximately 4.25 pounds of fruit annually. Haskap has a life expectancy of up to 30 years, so you'll have a long time to harvest from productive plants!

Haskap berries are ready for harvesting when they reach a deep blue colour with a faint white bloom (a pale smudge on the surface of the skin). If they are still green inside when broken open, it is too early to pick them. They should be red/purple inside when ready. Hand pick each individual berry (this is easier to do if growing cultivars with firm fruit) or manually shake the fruit from each shrub into an overturned umbrella or other shallow container placed on the ground beneath each plant.

One U-pick grower I met a few years ago had cut a keyhole shape into a large piece of corrugated foam board and slipped the board like a collar beneath the shrub. Folded flaps on every side of the board kept the berries from rolling onto the ground as we shook the shrubs to remove the fruit. When the board was covered in berries, we just tilted the contents into our pails. Be sure to wear gloves while picking haskap berries, or you'll come away with purple-stained hands! Always harvest on a cool morning. Haskap berries will rapidly become mushy if picked in the heat of the day.

Some cultivars have softer berries than others, and breeders are constantly working on creating plants with firmer berries so that they are more suitable to commercial growing. Haskap berries should not be stacked on top of each other as the pressure from the uppermost berries may crush the lower fruit. Baskets should be shallow so that the berries can sit in one layer.

The dark blue berries may be oval to cylindrical in shape, depending on the cultivar. Multiple seeds (up to 20) are found in each berry, but they are soft and barely noticeable when you chew them.

WHAT IS THE HASKAP BERRY FLAVOUR LIKE?

Haskap berries are seriously juicy, and rather tart, with a taste reminiscent of a mash-up between raspberries and blueberries. Some gardeners prefer not to eat them out of hand but consider haskap jam the ultimate delicacy. I love them either way . . . and many more, besides!

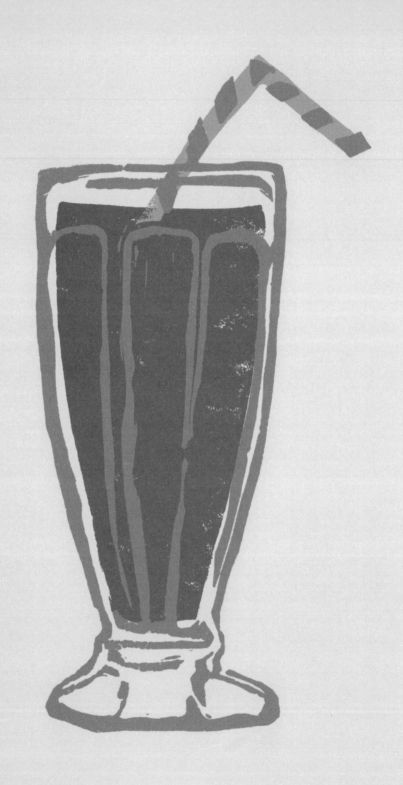

Haskap Berry and Banana Breakfast Shake

DF V VG — *Makes two 10-ounce drinks*

If crawling out of bed in the morning and going to work is absolutely necessary (why, oh why?), then at least treat yourself to a breakfast shake that will make both your taste buds and tummy happy. This is it. If you don't have tahini (sesame paste), almond or cashew butters are good substitutions.

2 cups cashew or almond milk
¾ cup fresh haskap berries
1 large banana, chopped
¼ cup dry quick oats
2 Tbsp tahini

Combine all ingredients in a blender and pulse until completely combined and smooth. Pour into two tall glasses and enjoy.

Haskap Berry and White Chocolate Scones

NF V — *Makes 12 scones* — Swap: Saskatoons for the haskap berries

High tea? Check. A grab-and-go breakfast? Check. Midnight snack? Check. These fruity, chocolatey scones are suitable for all occasions. They freeze beautifully (for up to 1 month) and can be quickly warmed in the microwave or toaster oven. I haven't hit on a gluten-free flour blend that rises sufficiently to give these the oomph needed, so I would recommend using only all-purpose flour for this recipe. Otherwise, you may end up making fruity, chocolatey triangular hockey pucks!

2 cups all-purpose flour, plus additional flour for rolling out the dough

¼ cup granulated sugar

2½ tsp baking powder

¼ tsp kosher salt

6 Tbsp cold unsalted butter, cut into cubes

½ cup low-fat milk

1 egg, lightly beaten

1½ cups frozen haskap berries

½ cup white chocolate chips

1. Preheat the oven to 400°F.

2. Line a baking sheet with a piece of parchment paper.

3. Mix the flour, sugar, baking powder, and salt in a large bowl. Using your fingers, rub the butter into the flour mixture until it resembles coarse crumbs. Add the milk and egg. Stir the mixture just until combined. Fold in the haskap berries and the chocolate chips. The dough will be soft.

4. Sprinkle some flour onto a work surface, and roll the dough out into a 1-inch-thick rectangle. Cut the large rectangle into 6 smaller ones, then cut each rectangle diagonally into 2 triangles.

5. Place the scones on the prepared baking sheet. Bake them in the oven for 20 minutes.

6. Remove the scones from the oven and serve them warm.

Haskap Berry Peanut Energy Bites

DF V VG — *Makes approximately 14* — Swap: Saskatoons or currants for haskap berries

Energy bites have huge value as lunch box staples, in-the-car or at-the-soccer-game snacks, or high-protein hiking grub. Easy to make and even easier to eat, this particular recipe literally pops with every bite of tangy haskap berries. I do not recommend allowing the frozen berries to thaw before rolling the dough into balls—otherwise, you'll end up with purple energy bites and stained hands from the juice. You might be okay with that, though, so I will leave it up to you.

½ cup creamy peanut butter   ½ cup chopped peanuts
2 Tbsp maple syrup   ⅓ cup frozen haskap berries (not thawed)
1 cup quick oats

1. Place a piece of parchment paper on a baking sheet.

2. Combine the peanut butter and the maple syrup in a medium bowl. Add the oats, peanuts, and haskap berries and mix thoroughly.

3. Using your hands, roll approximately 2 Tbsp of the dough into a ball. Place the ball on the prepared baking sheet. Repeat this step with the remaining dough.

4. Place the baking sheet in the refrigerator and chill for at least 30 minutes. The energy balls are now ready to eat! Store them in the refrigerator for up to 1 week.

Haskap Berry Soup

GF NF V — *Makes 4 servings*

In Sweden, there is a tradition of eating blueberry or bilberry soup—either warm or chilled and sometimes for breakfast! A few years ago, I started eating blueberry soup to gain a few healthy antioxidants and vitamins at the start of the day and discovered that it is unbelievably soothing for the ol' digestive system. If blueberry soup is good, shouldn't haskap berry soup be better? Yup—it certainly is! The tangy berries elevate this fruit soup to a flavour experience that everyone should wake up to in the morning. (You don't have to eat this at breakfast, however—consider serving it as a first course to a meal of roasted meat or baked fish).

3 cups fresh or frozen haskap berries
2 cups plus 1 Tbsp cold water, divided
¼ cup honey
1 Tbsp lemon juice

¼ tsp cinnamon
2 Tbsp ground flaxseed
2 Tbsp plain yogurt

1. Combine the haskap berries, 2 cups water, honey, lemon juice, and cinnamon in a large saucepan. Over high heat bring the mixture to a boil, then turn the heat down to medium. Simmer the soup for 5 minutes.

2. In the meantime, mix the 1 Tbsp of cold water and flaxseed in a small cup. Add it to the soup and stir.

3. Remove the soup from the heat. Cool it for 10 minutes, then stir in the yogurt.

4. Serve immediately.

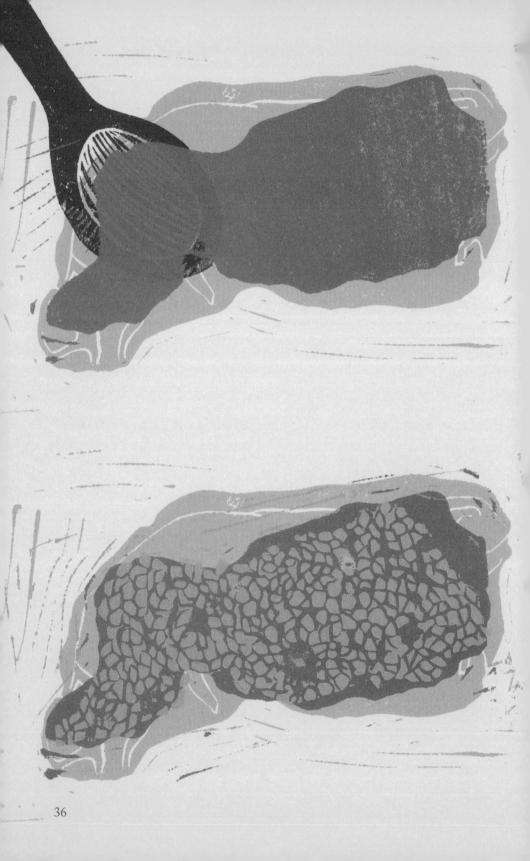

Pork Chops with Haskap Berry Topping

NF — *Makes 4 pork chops*

There are a couple of big reasons to love this recipe—besides the great taste! First of all, the meat isn't fried, which is good for those of us who shouldn't eat fried foods. Secondly, the mixture of juicy haskap berries and mustard is hugely complementary to the pork, and it keeps the meat tender. (We've all had dry, chewy pork chops—you'll never have that problem again if you cook them this way.) Panko bread crumbs are Japanese in origin, but they are easily found in any grocery store. They are made from white bread but don't contain the crusts of the bread, like regular bread crumbs do. They are crunchy and light in texture and ideal for breading or topping meat, fish, and poultry.

4 boneless pork chops
1 Tbsp unsalted butter
½ cup panko-style bread crumbs
¼ cup fresh haskap berries, crushed

1 Tbsp Dijon mustard
1 tsp extra-virgin olive oil
Kosher salt and ground black pepper, to taste

1. Preheat the oven to 375°F.

2. Place a piece of parchment paper on a baking sheet. Lay the pork chops on top of the parchment.

3. In a small skillet, melt the butter over medium heat. Add the bread crumbs and mix. Toast them lightly, stirring frequently, for about 2 minutes. They will turn golden brown. Remove them from the heat and set them aside.

4. In a small bowl, combine the haskap berries, the Dijon mustard, the olive oil, and the salt and pepper. Divide this mixture and spread it evenly over the top of each pork chop.

5. Spoon the toasted bread crumbs evenly over the top of each pork chop, covering the haskap berry topping.

6. Bake the pork chops in the prepared oven for 20 minutes or until the pork chops are done. If your pork chops are really thick, you may need to increase the baking time.

7. Serve the chops with sautéed garden-fresh vegetables and hot steamed rice.

Haskap Berry Chocolate Bark

GF NF V VG — *Makes 4 ounces* — Swap: Saskatoons for the haskap berries

This recipe can be easily doubled (or tripled!) if you're making the bark as gifts. Yeah, gifts ... *right*. Because the fruit is fresh instead of dried, the bark should be stored in the fridge and gobbled down within 3 days of making it. Don't worry; it won't be a difficult task to accomplish.

¼ cup raw, hulled, unsalted pumpkin seeds
4 ounces semi-sweet chocolate
¼ cup fresh haskap berries
Pinch of fine sea salt

1. Place the pumpkin seeds in a blender and pulse once or twice until they are coarsely chopped.

2. Heat the chocolate on low heat over a double boiler on the stovetop until it is completely melted. (See facing page for instructions on how to make a double boiler.) This takes about 5 to 7 minutes. Remove the chocolate from the heat.

3. Place a piece of parchment paper on a baking sheet. Using a spatula, spread the chocolate in a ¼-inch layer in the middle of the sheet. (There won't be enough chocolate to cover the surface of the entire baking sheet.)

4. Sprinkle the chopped pumpkin seeds and haskap berries over the chocolate. They should sink into the chocolate a bit. Sprinkle the salt over the chocolate.

5. Place the baking sheet, uncovered, in the refrigerator and chill for at least 4 hours. Break the bark up into large chunks and enjoy! Store the bark in an airtight container.

HOW TO MAKE A DOUBLE BOILER
TO MELT CHOCOLATE AND TO SCALD MILK

Milk scalds at a temperature of 180°F. Before pasteurization was commonplace, milk was scalded to kill bacteria. We still scald milk for custards as it helps to dissolve the sugar in the recipe and minimizes the curdling of eggs. While you can melt chocolate or scald milk using a microwave, this old-school method is almost as easy (and you don't have to keep opening the door of the microwave to check on it).

1. You'll need two saucepans—a large one, and one that fits just inside the bigger one.

2. Fill the larger saucepan with about 1½ inches of water. Bring the water to a simmer.

3. Measure the chocolate or milk into the smaller saucepan. Place the saucepan into the larger saucepan over the simmering water. Just make sure that the bottom of the smaller pan is not touching the boiling water. Turn the heat down if necessary to maintain the water at a simmer.

4. Melt the chocolate or heat the milk. Stir frequently; in the case of the chocolate, it will help you determine when the chocolate is fully melted, and with the milk, it will prevent that icky skin of proteins forming on the surface.

5. When the chocolate or milk is ready, remove it from the heat and use it in your recipe.

Haskap Berry and Beet
Dark Chocolate Brownies

NF — *Makes about 16 brownies*

If the addition of beets to brownies renders a "healthier" version of this delectable chocolate treat, then the combination of haskap berries + beets + dark chocolate must make these brownies a certified nutritional powerhouse! Well . . . maybe not, but your taste buds will be thrilled with you anyway.

½ cup unsalted butter, melted

1 cup granulated sugar

2 eggs

½ cup cooked and puréed beets

½ cup all-purpose flour

⅓ cup Dutch processed cocoa

¾ cup fresh or frozen haskap berries

½ cup dark chocolate chips

1. Preheat the oven to 350°F.

2. Place a piece of baking parchment into an 9- × 9-inch baking pan.

3. In a large bowl, combine the butter and sugar. Add the eggs and the beets. Stir to mix thoroughly. Fold in the flour and cocoa. Add the haskap berries and chocolate chips and mix just until combined. Spread the batter in the prepared pan.

4. Bake 30 to 35 minutes or until a tester inserted into the centre of the batter comes out clean. Cool the brownies in the pan on a wire rack for at least 20 minutes.

5. Serve warm with a generous dollop of vanilla bean–flecked ice cream.

Haskap Berry Crisp

NF V — *Makes four 8-ounce ramekins* — Swap: Saskatoons or sour cherries for haskap berries

Everyone needs (yes, *needs!*) a good basic fruit crisp recipe in their baking arsenal, and this perfectly fits the bill. The tangy flavour of the haskap berries is front and centre in this easy, quick dessert, but if you want to add spices, experiment with cardamom, cinnamon, cloves, ginger, or nutmeg—or perhaps a combination.

½ cup unsalted butter, melted, plus
  additional butter for greasing ramekins
3 cups fresh or frozen haskap berries
¾ cup brown sugar, divided

1½ cups quick oats
½ cup all-purpose flour
Pinch of kosher salt

1. Preheat the oven to 350°F.

2. Grease four 8-ounce oven-safe ramekins with butter.

3. In a medium bowl, combine the haskap berries and ¼ cup brown sugar. Divide the mixture between the four ramekins.

4. In a large bowl, mix together the oats, flour, ½ cup brown sugar, and salt. Add the melted butter, and combine until the mixture resembles coarse crumbs. Divide the crumb mixture evenly over the top of the fruit in the four ramekins.

5. Bake the crisp in the oven for 25 minutes.

6. Remove the ramekins from the oven, and allow them to cool for 15 minutes before serving them with a dollop of whipped cream or vanilla ice cream. Or both.

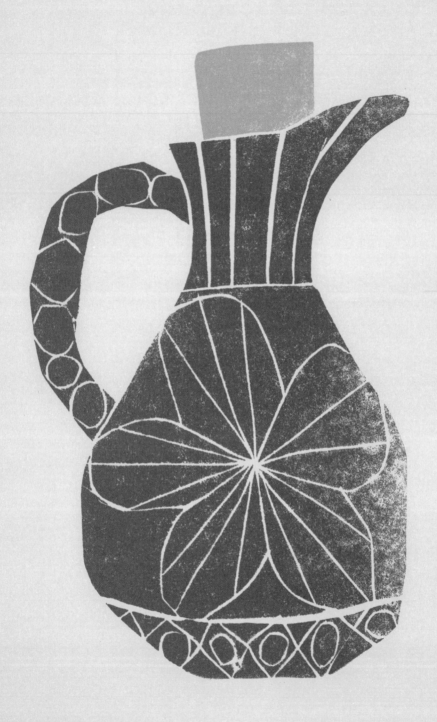

Haskap Berry Vinaigrette

GF DF NF V VG — *Makes 1 cup of dressing* — Swap: Saskatoons or currants for haskap berries

A fresh green salad featuring lettuce and other crisp vegetables from your garden or local greenhouse is a starter dish that goes with nearly every meal; it's also perfect for lunch with some added protein, such as chopped chicken or scrambled tofu. Of course, you'll be needing a dressing to go with that—and this tangy haskap berry vinaigrette is chock full of good-for-you ingredients. Pour the vinaigrette over a salad comprised of leaf lettuce or mixed spring greens, cucumber, radishes, celery, tomatoes, and scallions. It's a win-win!

½ cup haskap berry juice (see page 15 for how to juice berries)

2 Tbsp balsamic vinegar

1 Tbsp maple syrup

2 tsp fresh lemon juice

¼ tsp Dijon mustard

Kosher salt and ground black pepper, to taste

¼ cup olive oil

Combine the haskap berry juice, the balsamic vinegar, the maple syrup, the lemon juice, the mustard, and the salt and pepper in a small bowl. Drizzle in the olive oil and whisk all the ingredients together.

Haskap Berry Jam with Vanilla Bean and Cardamom

GF DF NF V VG — *Makes 2 half-pint jars*

Did you know that vanilla beans are produced by a specific type of orchid? Whole vanilla beans can sometimes be a challenge to obtain, and they may be a bit expensive to purchase, so feel free to substitute 2 tablespoons of very good vanilla extract (that means it's not artificial!) for the vanilla bean in this recipe.

And what about black cardamom? This highly fragrant spice from the ginger family is commonly used in Indian cooking, and it is more intensely flavoured than the green cardamom usually used for baked goods. If black cardamom pods are not available for you to use, ground cardamom (which is likely green cardamom unless it is marked otherwise) will do in a pinch— just add 2 teaspoons of it to this recipe.

If you're not at all keen on the extra zing the cardamom and vanilla add to this recipe, you can omit them entirely for a perfect version of pure haskap jam.

1 whole vanilla bean
2 black cardamom pods
4 cups haskap berries

1 cup granulated sugar
3 Tbsp orange juice

1. Follow all of the instructions on page 18 to sterilize and prepare your canning jars, screw bands, and sealing discs.

2. Slice the vanilla bean lengthwise and scrape out the seeds. Add the bean pod and the seeds to a large saucepan.

3. Using a nutcracker, crack the cardamom pods so that they slightly open, but do not remove the seeds. Place the opened pods into the saucepan.

4. Add the haskap berries, the sugar, and the orange juice to the saucepan. Bring the mixture to a boil over high heat.

5. Turn the heat down to medium-low, and boil for approximately 20 minutes, or until the candy thermometer test (see page 21) shows that the jam has reached the gel point.

6. Take the jam off the heat. Remove the vanilla bean and cardamom pods and discard them. Pour the jam into the prepared jars, and process it according to the instructions on page 18.

There are approximately 20 species of saskatoons found in North America, but the best-known one in Canada is *Amelanchier alnifolia*, found growing wild over nearly all parts of the prairie provinces and elsewhere in the country. Cultivated shrubs bred from this parent—and others in the genus—dot urban and rural residential landscapes alike and the fruit from them are staple offerings of many U-pick farms. Despite the fact that saskatoons are fairly common, many gardeners treat them as ornamentals and miss out on a uniquely delicious berry that is hugely versatile in cooking and baking.

This is one of my favourite shrubs for so many reasons: the serrated, oval leaves turn reddish-orange in the fall and gorgeous sprays of pure white flowers appear in early spring. The purple berries are borne on slightly pendulous clusters. Their growth habit is upright, fairly tidy, and, overall, quite appealing. The shrubs can sucker, however, so be prepared to remove or transplant root sprouts if necessary. Some gardeners successfully employ the shrubs as hedges, planting them in snug rows.

CULTIVATING SASKATOONS

Saskatoons fare best when in well-drained, loamy soil rich in organic matter, but they will pretty much perform in any soil conditions except in a bog. A location in full sun is a must for optimal fruit production. Ensure the site you select has minimal exposure to drying winds year-round, and receives high heat in the summer. Situating your saskatoons at the base of a slope is a big no-no, as the resulting frost pocket may damage the early spring blooms if temperatures dip.

Plant saskatoons in the spring or fall. If you choose to do the job in the fall, be sure to allow enough time before the ground freezes for the shrubs to establish good root systems.

Maintain a regular, consistent watering schedule if rainfall is not sufficient throughout the growing season. Although saskatoons are fairly drought tolerant once established, they will benefit from supplemental irrigation in times of need. Just before the berries are ready to harvest, stop watering for a few days—many gardeners swear that this improves the flavour of the fruit.

Apply a side dressing of about 1 to 2 inches of compost annually in early spring, around the time that the plants are beginning to flower. No additional amendments of fertilizer are necessary for the rest of the year.

Keep weeds to a minimum to prevent them from stealing nutrients and water from the shrubs. Mulching with a layer of clean, weed-free straw can help keep the weeds to a dull roar and conserve moisture during times of low rainfall.

The precision of any pruning you undertake is critical, as saskatoons bear fruit on the previous year's wood (and older). Remove branches that are the least productive—those older than four years. (This means you won't prune for the first few years of growth.) Dead or diseased branches may be removed at any time. Pruning should be undertaken in early spring before the shrub breaks dormancy. Do not remove more than 25 percent of the branches in a growing season to minimize the risk of stress on the plant. As the shrub ages and becomes slightly overgrown, it may be given a rejuvenation prune, back to ground level. Bear in mind that this will set fruit production back for several more years!

PESTS AND DISEASES

Some fungal leaf spots afflict saskatoons, but they are generally a cosmetic issue more than a deadly one. Do not use heavy nitrogen fertilizers, which can promote lush vegetative growth that may encourage leaf spots to develop. Make sure that you water the base of the plants and not up into the foliage, which may facilitate the spread of spores. Clean up all leaf litter and fallen berries from beneath the shrubs.

Saskatoon-juniper rust is a common problem for saskatoons (and junipers!). This interesting fungus requires two hosts, one from the Rose family and one from the Juniper family, to complete its life cycle. On a saskatoon plant, you might see blackened tissue on the leaves or black lesions on the berries. The berries might be misshapen as well. Eventually, you'll see red spiky spores form on the berries. There are fungicides available to treat saskatoon-juniper rust, but the easiest, most organic way to prevent the problem is through siting. Don't plant saskatoons and junipers in close proximity, and you won't have an issue.

THE FRUIT!

Saskatoons will take approximately 4 years from planting to begin fruit production and peak about 3 years later. Healthy plants can bear fruit for 30 years or more. The berries are a midsummer treat, ready in July over a few short weeks. Look for a dark purple (almost black) colour—if they are still green or reddish-pink, they are not ready yet. They should no longer be rock hard to the touch. Saskatoon berries tend to ripen all at once, so nearly the whole crop can be easily harvested over a few days. The berries are sweet, but not generously so; they have an almond-like flavour. The tiny seeds inside give them a nut-like feel as well, although they are quite soft.

Saskatoon Berry Carrot Muffins

NF DF V — *Makes 12 large muffins*

Right around the time you are ready to harvest saskatoons, the first decent-sized carrots will be coming on in your garden. These two ingredients are a match made in heaven! These muffins are ideal lunch box companions. They freeze very well for up to 1 month.

1½ cups coarsely grated carrots

¼ cup brown sugar

½ cup granulated sugar

⅓ cup sunflower or safflower oil

1 large egg

1 cup all-purpose flour

½ cup quick oats

½ tsp baking soda

½ tsp ground cinnamon

½ tsp ground nutmeg

¼ tsp baking powder

¼ tsp kosher salt

1 cup fresh or frozen saskatoons

1. Preheat the oven to 350°F.

2. Line a muffin pan with parchment paper cups.

3. Combine the carrots, brown sugar, granulated sugar, oil, and egg in a medium bowl and stir.

4. Mix the flour, oats, baking soda, cinnamon, nutmeg, baking powder, and salt in a separate large bowl.

5. Add the wet ingredients to the dry ingredients and stir until combined.

6. Fold in the saskatoons.

7. Divide the batter evenly among the paper cups in the muffin pan.

8. Bake in the oven for 20 minutes or until a tester inserted in the centre of the muffins comes out clean. Cool in the muffin pan on a wire rack. These muffins can be enjoyed warm or at room temperature.

Roasted Asparagus with Saskatoon Berry Dressing

GF DF NF V — *Makes 2 servings of 6 asparagus spears each*

There is a farm in central Alberta that offers tours of their asparagus fields during harvest time in the spring. Asparagus still isn't widely grown on the prairies, and certainly not as a commercial endeavour, so it's exciting to see rows and rows of green (and purple) spears poking out of the ground like weird fingers. The best part of the tour is going out into the field to snap a fresh spear out of the warm soil, to munch on right there in the sunshine. And, of course, my husband and I always come home with bundles of newly harvested and chilled asparagus, purchased at the farm store. While it's delightful on its own, elevating this delicious vegetable with a saskatoon berry dressing is even better. *Do it.*

ASPARAGUS
12 asparagus spears
2 Tbsp olive oil

DRESSING
½ cup fresh saskatoons
2 Tbsp balsamic vinegar
2 Tbsp honey
1 Tbsp extra-virgin olive oil
1 tsp garlic, crushed
Pinch of kosher salt
Pinch of ground black pepper

1. Preheat the oven to 425°F.

2. Cover a rimmed baking sheet with a piece of parchment paper.

3. Wash the asparagus and trim the bottoms of the spears. Lay the asparagus spears on the baking sheet and drizzle the olive oil over top.

4. Roast the asparagus in the preheated oven for 12 to 15 minutes or until it is tender-crisp.

5. In the meantime, combine all of the dressing ingredients in a small bowl.

6. Remove the asparagus from the oven and put on a serving plate. Spoon the dressing over the asparagus.

Saskatoon Berry Barbecue Sauce

GF DF NF V VG — *Makes 2 cups* — Swap: Haskap berries, currants, or sour cherries for saskatoons

Whether you're grilling bison, elk, beef, pork, chicken, or a vegetarian burger, this tangy/garlicky/smoky barbecue sauce is the perfect condiment to accompany it.

1 Tbsp extra-virgin olive oil

1 small shallot, finely minced

3 small garlic cloves, crushed

3 cups fresh or frozen saskatoons

½ cup brown sugar, packed

½ cup ketchup

¼ cup maple syrup

1 Tbsp apple cider vinegar

2 tsp ground black pepper

1 tsp kosher salt

1 tsp smoked paprika

½ tsp ground mustard

2 Tbsp fresh lemon juice

1. Warm the olive oil in a large saucepan over low heat. Add the shallot and garlic. Sauté until golden brown, about 10 minutes.

2. Add the remaining ingredients except for the lemon juice to the saucepan. Bring the mixture to a boil, then turn the heat down to low. Simmer, stirring occasionally, for 45 minutes. The mixture will thicken and reduce slightly.

3. Add the lemon juice and remove the sauce from the heat. Cool the mixture to room temperature. Purée the mixture with an immersion blender until smooth.

4. Saskatoon berry barbecue sauce may be kept in the refrigerator in a sealed jar for up to 1 month.

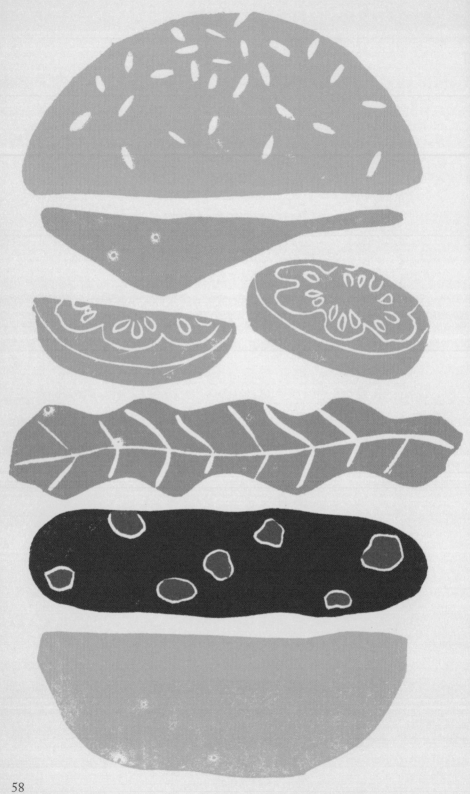

Chicken and Saskatoon Berry Burgers

DF NF — *Makes 8 burgers* — Swap: Sour cherries or currants for the saskatoons

Berries in your chicken burgers? The wild, sweet taste of saskatoons elevates these lean chicken burgers to a new level and keeps them moist. If you don't want to fry the burgers, you can grill them on the barbecue instead. Serve these burgers with freshly baked buns and all the trimmings: garden-fresh tomato slices, lettuce leaves, and an aged cheddar cheese.

1 Tbsp extra-virgin olive oil
1 lb ground chicken
½ cup frozen saskatoons
¼ cup quick oats
2 garlic cloves, minced

2 green onions, chopped
1 Tbsp soy sauce
Salt and ground black pepper, to taste

1. Heat the olive oil in a large skillet over medium heat.

2. Combine the chicken, saskatoons, oats, garlic, green onions, soy sauce, and salt and pepper in a large bowl. Using your hands, make 8 patties from the meat mixture.

3. Place the patties in the hot oil and fry for about 7 minutes. Turn the patties and fry for another 5 minutes, or until the burgers are cooked thoroughly.

Saskatoon Berry Meat Pie

DF NF — *Makes one 9-inch pie*

I had never eaten—much less heard of—tourtière until I met my husband. His French-Canadian mother was an expert at making her special version of this ground meat pie, and I was enamoured with the dish as soon as I had my very first bite. Fast forward many years (I won't divulge exactly how many), and I got to thinking: Saskatoon dessert pies are a huge treat among berry lovers, so why not marry the wild sweet flavour of the fruit with pork and beef and assemble it in the heartiest example of comfort food you've ever had the pleasure of enjoying? (I've changed up Mom's spice mixture and made a few other tweaks to complement the saskatoons, but her pie remains the inspiration!)

FILLING

1 lb lean ground pork

8 oz lean ground beef

1 medium onion, finely diced

1 cup fresh or frozen saskatoons

½ cup water

1 tsp kosher salt

¼ tsp ground thyme

¼ tsp ground sage

¼ tsp ground black pepper

CRUST

2½ cups all-purpose flour

½ tsp kosher salt

¼ cup cold vegetable shortening, cut into cubes

⅔ cup ice water, divided

1. First make the filling. Combine all the filling ingredients in a large saucepan. Cook over medium heat, stirring occasionally, until mixture comes to a simmer. Reduce heat to low and simmer until meat is cooked, between 5 and 10 minutes. Remove the mixture from the heat, and allow it to cool to room temperature before using it to fill the pie.

2. To make the pie crust, mix the flour and the salt in a large bowl. Work in the shortening with your fingers, until the mixture resembles coarse cornmeal.

3. Add ⅓ cup of water to start. Mix the dough with your hands until it comes together into a ball. If you need to, add more water (but no more than ⅔ cup, total).

4. Divide the dough in half. Flatten each dough section into a disc and cover in plastic wrap. Refrigerate them for 30 minutes.

5. Remove the dough discs from the refrigerator, and let them sit for 5 to 10 minutes. (This will make it easier to roll out the dough.)

6. When you're ready to assemble the pie, preheat the oven to 425°F.

7. On a floured work surface, roll out one of the discs until it is about 12 inches in diameter. Lay the lower pie crust into the bottom of a 9-inch pie pan.

8. Spoon the cooled filling into the bottom crust. Roll out the second disc of dough. Carefully place the top pie crust over the filling to cover it. Crimp the edges of the pie crusts to seal the pie, and cut away any excess pie dough.

9. Cut some slits in the top crust of the pie to allow the steam to vent. Cover the edges of the pie with an aluminum foil shield (see note below).

10. Bake the pie in the preheated oven for 20 minutes. Remove the aluminum foil strips and continue baking the pie for another 15 to 20 minutes, or until the crust is golden brown.

11. Remove the pie from the oven. Allow it to cool for about 10 minutes before serving.

HOW TO MAKE AN ALUMINUM FOIL PIE SHIELD

Pie crusts often darken or even burn on the edges, and that is simply no good at all. Protect the crust with a shield made of aluminum foil. You can always seek out fancier methods online, and you can even purchase sturdy, reusable pie shields made from aluminum, but this is a quick, no-fuss way to do it: Tear off five 3-inch-wide strips of aluminum foil. Place each strip so that it covers the edges of the pie crust. The strips will overlap. Curl them around the edge of the crust so that they remain in place.

Saskatoon Berry Cake

NF V — *Makes one 9- × 12-inch cake*

This cake is versatile enough to pack for school or work lunches and special enough to take to a friend's house for a coffee date. The oat flour enhances the almond flavour of the saskatoons. If you don't have oat flour on hand, you can make your own by grinding quick oats in a blender. (I actually use a coffee grinder that has never seen coffee beans.) Substituting all-purpose flour will work, as well.

CAKE
⅓ cup unsalted butter, softened
2 Tbsp vegetable oil
½ cup granulated sugar
2 large eggs
1 tsp vanilla
1½ cups oat flour
1 tsp baking powder
1 tsp ground cardamom (optional)

½ tsp kosher salt
½ cup sour cream
3 cups fresh or frozen saskatoons

STREUSEL TOPPING
½ cup brown sugar
½ cup oat flour
¼ cup unsalted butter, softened

1. Preheat the oven to 350°F. Cut a piece of parchment paper to line a 9- × 12-inch pan.

2. Make the cake batter first. In a large bowl with a hand-held or stand mixer, beat the butter, vegetable oil, sugar, eggs, and vanilla.

3. In a medium bowl, mix the oat flour, baking powder, cardamom (if using), and salt.

4. Add the dry ingredients to the liquid ingredients. Stir to combine. Add the sour cream and stir until incorporated. Fold in the berries.

5. Mix the streusel ingredients in a separate small bowl until they resemble coarse crumbs.

6. Pour the cake batter into the prepared cake pan. Sprinkle the streusel on top of the batter.

7. Bake the cake in the preheated oven for 75 minutes or until a tester inserted into the centre of the cake comes out clean.

8. Remove the cake from the oven, and set the pan on a rack to cool. The cake may be served warm or cold. Store leftovers in an airtight container in the refrigerator for up to 3 days. The cake may be frozen for up to 2 months.

Saskatoon Berry Cream Puffs

NF V — *Makes 12 cream puffs*

Airy, delicate, and filled with fruity whipped cream—these cream puffs may look daunting but they're absolutely not. *Trust me.* These use a very small amount of saskatoon juice, so if you want a little bit more berry flavour, mix ¼ cup fresh saskatoon berries into the filling. This will make the filling difficult to pipe, so it's best to use a spoon to fill the pastries.

PASTRY
½ cup water
¼ cup unsalted butter
½ cup all-purpose flour
¼ tsp kosher salt
2 eggs

FILLING
½ cup whipping (35%) cream
1 Tbsp granulated sugar
1 Tbsp saskatoon juice (see page 15 for how to juice berries)

1. Preheat the oven to 375°F.

2. Place a piece of parchment paper on a baking sheet.

3. Start by preparing the pastry. Bring the water to a boil in a medium saucepan over high heat. Add the butter to the water and stir until the butter is melted. Add the flour and salt to the water and butter mixture and stir until the mixture forms a thick doughy ball.

4. Remove the saucepan from the heat. Using a hand-held or stand mixer, beat in one egg until the mixture is smooth. Let the dough sit for 5 minutes.

5. Add the other egg and beat until the mixture is creamy. Let the mixture stand for 10 minutes. Using a tablespoon, drop the dough in 12 mounds onto the prepared baking sheet. Give the puffs space on the sheetspacing them at least 2 inches apart.

6. Bake the cream puffs for 22 minutes or until the pastry is raised and a light golden brown. Do not check on them too soon, or the pastry may deflate. Depending on the size of the puffs and your oven, they may take up to 30 minutes to bake.

7. Remove the puffs from the oven and cool them completely on the baking sheet on a wire rack.

8. To make the filling, combine the whipping cream, the sugar, and the saskatoon juice in a large bowl. Using a standing or hand-held mixer, beat the mixture until it forms stiff peaks. This will take about 5 minutes.

9. Place the mixture into a piping bag (see below for creating a piping bag, if you don't own one). Using your fingers, gently break open a small hole in each puff. Pipe some filling into each puff.

10. These are ready to eat right away, or you can refrigerate them until ready to serve. They freeze well for up to 1 month.

HOW TO MAKE A SIMPLE PIPING BAG

If you don't have a piping bag, take a plastic bag with a zipper seal, and fill it with the pastry cream or icing. Close the seal. With a pair of scissors, snip one corner at the base of the bag. Don't cut off too much. This will give you a hole to pipe the pastry cream or icing from. Easy peasy!

Saskatoon Berry Trifle

NF V — *Makes two 1-pint Mason jars* — Swap: Substitute haskap berries or sour cherries for saskatoons

This recipe has many parts, but they're all easy to make, and they come together in a light, fresh dessert. Layer this pretty trifle into Mason pint jars and bring the dessert along to a summer barbeque. Always use fresh berries for this recipe—limp, thawed ones are just not as lovely. If 1-pint jars make too much dessert (is there such a thing, I wonder?), divide this between four half-pint jars instead.

CAKE
½ cup all-purpose flour
1 tsp baking powder
½ cup unsalted butter, softened
½ cup icing sugar
1 egg
½ tsp vanilla extract
¼ cup low-fat milk

PUDDING
1 cup low-fat milk, divided
3 Tbsp granulated sugar
2 Tbsp cornstarch
1 egg yolk
½ tsp vanilla extract

SASKATOON FILLING
1½ cups fresh saskatoons
2 Tbsp icing sugar

WHIPPED CREAM
½ cup (35%) whipping cream
1 Tbsp granulated sugar
1 Tbsp saskatoon berry juice (see page 15 for how to juice berries)

1. To make the cake, preheat the oven to 400°F.

2. Place a piece of parchment paper in a 9- × 5-inch loaf pan.

3. Combine the flour and the baking powder in a medium bowl and set aside.

4. Beat the butter and icing sugar with a hand-held or stand mixer in a large bowl until light and fluffy. Add the egg and the vanilla and beat until creamy.

5. Add the flour and baking powder mixture in two additions, alternating with the milk in two additions, to the butter and sugar mixture, stirring until just incorporated.

6. Spoon the batter into the prepared loaf pan.

7. Bake the cake in the oven for 20 minutes, or until a tester inserted in the centre of the cake comes out clean. Remove the cake from the oven and allow it to cool for 10 minutes, then remove it from the pan and cool it completely on a wire rack.

8. To prepare the pudding, put 3 Tbsp of cold milk into a cup and reserve. Scald the rest of the milk in a double boiler. (See page 39 for instructions on how to construct a double boiler.)

9. Add the sugar and the cornstarch to the 3 Tbsp milk in the cup. Stir until combined. Drizzle this mixture very slowly into the scalded milk, stirring constantly. Cook for about 5 minutes, over low heat, stirring frequently. The mixture should be smooth.

10. Add the egg yolk to the mixture. Cook the pudding for 2 more minutes, stirring constantly. The mixture will thicken up noticeably.

11. Remove the pudding from the heat and add the vanilla extract. Allow the pudding to cool completely, then refrigerate it until it is needed.

12. To make the saskatoon filling, combine the saskatoon berries and the icing sugar in a small bowl.

13. To prepare the whipped cream, combine the whipping cream, the sugar, and the berry juice in a large bowl. Beat the mixture with a hand-held or stand mixer on high speed, for about 5 minutes, or until the whipped cream forms stiff peaks.

14. To assemble the trifle, cut the cake into 4 pieces. Crumble one piece of cake into the bottom of each Mason jar.

15. Spoon ¼ of the pudding on top of the cake layer in each jar. Add ¼ of the saskatoon berries on top of the pudding layer in each jar. Crumble another piece of cake into each Mason jar. There won't be any more cake left after this step. Divide the rest of the pudding mixture between the two jars. Divide the remainder of the saskatoon berries between the two jars. Finally, top each Mason jar with the whipped cream! Then grab a spoon . . .

Saskatoon Berry and Apple Jelly

GF DF NF V VG — *Makes 3 half-pint jars*

Saskatoon berries do not have a lot of natural pectin, so if you don't want to use store-bought pectin, it helps to create some by pairing them with a fruit that is rich in natural pectin. Apples are that fruit!

APPLE PECTIN

4 apples, cut into quarters (no need to peel or core)

2 cups water

1 Tbsp fresh lemon juice

JELLY

2 cups saskatoon juice (see page 15 for how to juice berries)

1½ cups granulated sugar

2 tsp fresh lemon juice

1. To make the pectin, place the apples, the water, and the lemon juice into a large saucepan. Bring the mixture to a boil over high heat. Cover the saucepan. Lower the heat to medium and simmer the mixture for 20 minutes.

2. Remove the pan from the heat and allow it to cool. Strain the juice through layers of cheesecloth, a fine mesh sieve, or a jelly strainer.

3. To make the jelly, combine the apple pectin, the saskatoon juice, the sugar, and the lemon juice in a large saucepan. Bring the mixture to a boil. Reduce the heat to medium and simmer the mixture for 10 to 15 minutes, or until it reaches the gel point. (See page 21 for instructions on how to measure that with a candy thermometer.)

4. Pour the jam into the prepared jars and process it according to the instructions on page 18.

Saskatoon Berry Mint Cocktail

GF DF NF V VG — *Makes two 12-ounce drinks*

Mint is an incredibly low-maintenance plant—and a big-time spreader. If you plant it in the ground, even in our cold prairie climate, chances are you'll have an entire bed filled with it in a few years. Not necessarily a bad thing if you weren't planning on planting anything else there—and if you want mint to make fantastic drinks like this! (Seriously, though, if you want to control mint plants in the garden, plant them in a large container and sink the container into the ground right up to the rim. This will keep the plants confined to just one area.)

12 fresh mint leaves

½ cup simple syrup (see facing page for how to make simple syrup)

1 cup saskatoon juice (see page 15 for how to make saskatoon juice)

1 cup club soda or lime-flavoured sparkling water, divided

4 oz vodka

Juice of half a lime

1. Combine the mint leaves and the simple syrup in a small saucepan. Bring to a boil over high heat. Remove the syrup from the heat and allow it to cool to room temperature. Refrigerate it for at least 1 hour before using.

2. Fill two tall glasses with ice. Pour the mint syrup, saskatoon juice, vodka, and lime juice in a cocktail shaker. Shake to combine. Divide the mixture between the glasses and top each with ½ cup club soda or sparkling water. Use a stir stick to give the cocktail a quick whirl before taking that first refreshing sip.

NOTE: Omit the vodka for a fruity, non-alcoholic drink.

HOW TO MAKE A SIMPLE SYRUP

(makes approximately 1 cup)

Simple syrups are often used in cocktails as boiling the water and the sugar ensures that the sugar thoroughly dissolves. You don't want crystals of sugar in your drink! Make sure the simple syrup is completely cooled before using it in the cocktail of your choice. Leftover simple syrup can be placed in an airtight container and refrigerated for up to 1 week.

1 cup granulated sugar
1 cup water

Combine the sugar and the water in a saucepan. Bring the mixture to a boil over high heat. Turn the heat down to medium-high and stir until the sugar is completely dissolved. Remove the syrup from the heat. It is now ready to use to make a delicious drink!

CHOKECHERRIES

Native to the prairies and to much of Canada, chokecherries (*Prunus virginiana*) are cold-hardy, low-maintenance selections for small gardens. (They are sometimes considered a small shrub if multi-stemmed.) They can reach a height of 16 feet, and they have a tidy, upright form. In the wild, you'll find chokecherries growing over a wide range of ecosystems—in aspen-dominated forests, riparian areas, and skirting grasslands.

A common cultivar grown in many small urban yards and parklands in the prairie provinces is 'Schubert'. Bright green new leaves emerge in the spring and quickly change colour to a deep burgundy. While Schuberts are primarily grown for their ornamental value, the fruit they bear is just as edible as that of the species plants! Schubert chokecherries have a high propensity for suckering, so if you plant them, you will have to regularly remove these reproductive growths (if you don't want them, that is!). The original *P. virginiana* do not tend to sucker much.

HOW TO GROW CHOKECHERRIES

P. virginiana has dark green, oval-shaped, and heavily serrated leaves with pointed tips. The foliage turns bright yellow in autumn, adding another facet of ornamental appeal. Long racemes (clusters) of pure white flowers appear in late May through early June. The dark-coloured berries are initially green, turning red, and eventually nearly black. The berries appear in late summer, usually in August. The berries dangle from long pendulous trusses, in clusters of up to 12 berries or more.

Chokecherries are self-fertile, so only one plant is needed for fruit production. Bees go a bit gaga over the flowers in the spring, and you usually do not have to worry about a lack of pollination!

If you want heaps of chokecherries, plant the trees in full sun for maximum yield. Although chokecherries can tolerate part shade, a lack of sufficient air circulation can promote issues such as powdery mildew. Chokecherries are adaptable to a wide range of soil types, but excellent drainage is a must to discourage root rot, mould, and other problems. Watch when you are watering as well; chokecherries do not tolerate repeated bouts of overwatering. Maintain a consistent, regular watering schedule if the growing season is hot and dry.

Annually amend the soil in the spring with a side dressing of 1 to 2 inches of compost. Further applications of fertilizer are usually unnecessary.

Chokecherries generally don't require regular pruning. Occasionally, it may be necessary to thin branches if they become too dense. This can promote better air circulation in the canopy. Pruning to shape when it isn't really needed can actually open up the tree to a greater risk of contracting diseases like black knot or inviting insects to attack.

POTENTIAL PROBLEMS

Black knot is one of the most serious issues that can affect chokecherries. The disease is caused by a fungus called *Apiosporina morbosa*, and if you've seen it once, you'll immediately recognize it again, as it looks like an elongated, knobby glob of black tar stuck to a tree's branches. (Some gardeners say it resembles something a bit more scatological in nature, but this is a cookbook, so I'll try not to suppress your appetite.) The fungus eventually girdles affected branches and can, over time, destroy entire trees. It can affect trees in the wild as well as cultivated specimens and spreads rapidly via spores. Rainwater and supplemental irrigation can splash the spores up into the foliage of the tree. Failing to clean up and dispose of leaf litter from infected trees can also spread the disease.

To deal with black knot, carefully prune out infected branches at least 8 inches below the knot. It's best to do this task when the trees are dormant, in late autumn after leaf drop, or in early spring before leaf out. (As a bonus, the lack of leaves will expose the sites of the knots and help you determine where to cut.) Dispose of infected branches according to the regulations issued by your municipality. Do not compost them.

WHAT DO THEY TASTE LIKE?

Each chokecherry fruit contains a significant hard stone. The stones contain a small amount of the toxin cyanogenic glycoside amygdalin and should not be consumed (not to mention, they are smashingly bad for your teeth if you don't realize they are there). Combine this with the highly astringent (read: unpalatably sour!) flavour of the fruit, and you're not likely to eat chokecherries fresh off the tree. (Many species of birds consider them a delicacy, however.) Don't eat the fresh leaves or stems of the plant, either—they also contain the toxin.

As the stones are large and take up a generous amount of the berry's real estate, pitting the berries is not a viable option. For all of the chokecherry recipes in this book, I use juice (see page 15 for more information about how to juice berries).

Chokecherry Syrup

GF   DF   NF   V   VG — *Makes about 2½ cups of syrup*

It is essential to make at least one batch of syrup with your chokecherry harvest—you'll understand what I mean when you taste this drizzled over a stack of hot pancakes (see facing page for my favourite pancake recipe). I've given this recipe an extra bit of complexity by adding coconut sugar, but if you don't like the flavour of coconut, you could always use demerara sugar or even brown sugar instead.

2 cups chokecherry juice (see page 15 for how to juice berries)
1 cup coconut sugar

1. Combine the ingredients in a medium saucepan. Bring them to a boil over medium-high heat, then decrease the heat to low. Simmer the mixture for 10 minutes, stirring occasionally. Remove the syrup from the heat and allow it to cool to room temperature.

2. Pour the syrup into a clean glass bottle or jar and seal tightly. Store in the refrigerator and consume within 2 weeks.

Pancakes to Pour Chokecherry Syrup Over

NF V — *Makes 10 to 12 pancakes*

I have a deep abiding fondness for pancakes, and this slightly tuned version of my mum's recipe is the best there is, in my (only slightly) biased opinion. If you make these with gluten-free flour, reduce the baking powder to 2 teaspoons.

1½ cups all-purpose flour	1 egg
1 Tbsp granulated sugar	1¾ cups milk
3 tsp baking powder	2 Tbsp vegetable oil, plus more oil
½ tsp salt	for frying

1. Combine the flour, the sugar, the baking powder, and the salt in a batter bowl.

2. Beat the egg in a cup. Add it to the flour and sugar mixture.

3. Add the milk and the 2 Tbsp of vegetable oil and beat the batter until it is free of lumps.

4. Heat a skillet on medium heat. Add a splash of vegetable oil and swirl the skillet to coat the cooking surface.

5. Spoon generous spoonfuls of batter into the hot pan and cook the pancakes for 2 to 3 minutes, or until the surface of the pancakes start to bubble. Turn the pancakes over and cook them for another 2 to 3 minutes before removing them from the pan.

6. Repeat this step until all of the batter is used. Serve the pancakes piping hot—with chokecherry syrup, of course!

Tomato-Basil Buckwheat Salad with Chokecherry Dressing

GF NF V — *Makes 4 cups* — Swap: Currants for the chokecherries

You've probably eaten the ubiquitous summer salad containing fresh basil, home-grown tomatoes, and that delightfully firm cheese called bocconcini, but you've almost certainly never had it like this! I've elevated this summer salad several notches by adding protein-rich toasted buckwheat groats (also known as kasha) and a zippy dressing made from chokecherry juice and sweet honey. If you don't have buckwheat groats, you can use quinoa. Bulgur is another option, but it's not gluten free. It's time to celebrate the harvest!

SALAD
1 cup toasted buckwheat groats
1¾ cups water
1 Tbsp unsalted butter
10 large fresh basil leaves, cut in strips
2 large fresh tomatoes, diced
8 balls of bocconcini cheese, chopped

DRESSING
⅓ cup chokecherry juice (see page 15 for how to juice berries)
¼ cup honey
3 Tbsp extra-virgin olive oil
1 tsp kosher salt
1 tsp ground black pepper

1. Rinse and drain the buckwheat groats. Combine the buckwheat groats, water, and butter in a medium saucepan.

2. Bring the mixture to a boil, then reduce the heat and cover the pan with a lid. Cook the groats, stirring occasionally, for 18 minutes, or until all of the water is absorbed and the grains have softened.

3. Chill the buckwheat groats in the refrigerator for 2 hours.

4. Add the basil, diced tomatoes, and cheese to the buckwheat groats.

5. Combine all of the dressing ingredients in a small bowl. Add them to the buckwheat mixture and stir.

Baked Brie with Chokecherry Drizzle

GF V — *Makes one 20-ounce wheel of cheese* — Swap: Currants for the chokecherries

Two words: Yes, please.

One 20-ounce wheel of brie cheese
3 Tbsp maple syrup
2 Tbsp chokecherry juice (see page 15 for how to juice berries)
¼ cup chopped pecans

1. Preheat the oven to 350°F.

2. Place a piece of parchment paper inside a medium baking dish.

3. Set the brie inside the baking dish.

4. In a small bowl, combine the maple syrup and chokecherry juice. Drizzle it over the cheese. Sprinkle the chopped pecans on top.

5. Bake the cheese in the oven for 10 to 15 minutes or until it is light gold in colour. Serve it immediately with your favourite crackers.

Chokecherry Panna Cotta

GF NF — *Makes four 6-ounce ramekins* — Swap: Substitute currants for the chokecherries

Panna cotta ("cooked cream") is an Italian dessert that is insanely light and not excessively sweet. It sounds fancy and difficult to make, but it's actually very easy. Unflavoured gelatin can be found in the grocery store in the same aisle as Jell-O.

1½ cups half-and-half (12%)

½ cup chokecherry juice (see page 15 for how to juice berries)

¼ cup granulated sugar

3 Tbsp warm water

2½ tsp unflavoured gelatin

1. Combine the half-and-half, chokecherry juice, and sugar in a large saucepan. Bring the ingredients to a simmer over medium heat, stirring frequently to dissolve the sugar.

2. Remove the mixture from the heat and cover the saucepan with a lid. Let it sit at room temperature for 30 minutes.

3. Pour the warm water into a small bowl and add the gelatin powder, stirring to combine. Allow the gelatin mixture to sit for 5 minutes, then stir it into the cream and chokecherry juice mixture. Mix it well so that the gelatin is well-distributed, as this will help the panna cotta set properly.

4. Pour the panna cotta into four 6-ounce ramekins. Cover the ramekins with plastic wrap. Refrigerate the panna cotta for a minimum of 4 hours before serving.

Chokecherry Swirl Mini Cheesecakes

NF V — *Makes 6 mini cheesecakes* — Swap: Substitute currants for the chokecherries

If I don't want to make or eat an entire rich, decadent cheesecake, I make miniature ones. They bake quickly, they take less time to chill, and there's no need to prepare a water bath or anything fancy, which means they can arrive on my plate pronto. The swirl of chokecherry juice is more than just decoration. It adds a refreshing, tangy flavour.

GRAHAM CRACKER CRUST
⅓ cup graham cracker crumbs
1 Tbsp granulated sugar
1 Tbsp unsalted butter, melted

CHEESECAKE FILLING
8 oz full-fat cream cheese, softened
¼ cup granulated sugar
1 egg
6 Tbsp chokecherry juice, divided (see page 15 for how to juice berries)

1. Preheat the oven to 325°F.

2. In a small bowl, combine the graham cracker crumbs, 1 Tbsp granulated sugar, and the melted butter. Divide the mixture evenly between the compartments in a six-cup muffin tin. Press the graham cracker mixture firmly down into the base of the cups. Bake the crumb crust for 5 minutes. Remove the pan from the oven. Leave the oven on.

3. With a hand-held or stand mixer, mix the cream cheese and the ¼ cup granulated sugar until smooth. Add the egg and beat until thoroughly combined.

4. Divide the cream cheese mixture evenly between the cups of the muffin tin, spooning it on top of the graham cracker crusts.

5. Pour 1 Tbsp of chokecherry juice into the centre of each unbaked cheesecake. With the tip of a toothpick, swirl the chokecherry juice through the cream cheese mixture.

6. Bake the cheesecakes in the oven for 25 minutes.

7. Remove the cheesecakes from the oven and allow them to cool to room temperature. Carefully remove cheesecakes from the muffin tin and chill them in the refrigerator for at least 2 hours before serving.

Chokecherry Chutney

GF DF NF V VG — *Makes about 2 cups* — Swap: Substitute currants for chokecherries

Forget boiled cranberry sauce. *This* is your new Thanksgiving or Christmas side for roasted turkey, guaranteed! It's even better when added to leftover chicken or turkey sandwiches. Or try it spooned over grilled pork chops. You could also warm up some delectable brie cheese and serve the chutney on the side. Or, really, just gobble it out of the bowl . . .

½ cup chokecherry juice (see page 15 for how to juice berries)

2 medium apples, cored and diced

½ cup brown sugar

½ cup golden raisins

¼ cup apple cider vinegar

¼ tsp red pepper flakes

¼ tsp ground cloves

½ tsp kosher salt

1. Combine all the ingredients in a large saucepan.

2. Simmer the ingredients over medium heat for about 10 minutes, stirring occasionally, or until the apples soften.

3. Remove the chutney from the heat. Cover it and chill it in the refrigerator for at least 4 hours before serving. This will keep in the fridge for up to 2 weeks, but you'll eat it all before then.

Chokecherry Pudding Cake

NF V — *Makes 1 cake* — Swap: Substitute currants for the chokecherries

This recipe is a riff on a traditional "half hour" pudding and features the slightly nerve-wracking practice of pouring a bunch of boiling liquid on top of a soft dough. Don't worry; it bakes up into something special, particularly with the addition of the flavourful chokecherry juice! Unfortunately, substituting a gluten-free flour blend doesn't work in this recipe; the gluten in the flour is essential to help make the pudding and prevent the cake from becoming rubbery. This cake should be made the way it is written.

CAKE

1 tsp unsalted butter, softened, to grease the pan

1 cup all-purpose flour

⅓ cup brown sugar

2 tsp baking powder

½ cup low-fat milk

SAUCE

1 cup water

1 cup chokecherry juice (see page 15 for how to juice berries)

1 cup brown sugar

1 Tbsp unsalted butter

1. Preheat the oven to 350°F.

2. Grease a 7- × 11-inch baking pan with 1 tsp of butter.

3. Make the cake first. Combine the flour, the ⅓ cup of brown sugar, and the baking powder in a medium bowl. Add the milk and stir until a soft dough is formed. Spoon the dough into the prepared baking dish.

4. In a medium saucepan, combine all of the sauce ingredients. Bring the mixture to a boil over high heat, and stir until the butter is melted. Remove the sauce from the stovetop and carefully pour it over the cake batter in the baking dish.

5. Place the baking dish in the preheated oven and bake for 25 minutes, or until the cake is no longer runny. You'll notice that as the cake baked, the batter moved from the bottom of the pan and it now rests on top of the pudding.

6. Remove the cake from the oven and cool for 20 minutes. Serve warm with ice cream or whipped cream.

Chokecherry Rosewater Jelly

GF DF NF V — *Makes 3 quarter-pint jars*

This small-batch recipe includes a splash of an ingredient common in Middle Eastern cooking: rosewater. You can usually find bottles of this fragrant and flavourful infused water in the international aisle of large grocery stores. If you don't have rosewater, or you simply want to make an excellent chokecherry jelly without any added flavours, omit that extra ingredient. Regardless, this is a favourite way to enjoy tangy chokecherries!

1 cup chokecherry juice (see page 15 for how to juice berries)

1½ cups granulated sugar

1 oz powdered pectin (this is half of a standard 2 oz package)

1½ tsp fresh lemon juice

1 tsp rosewater

1. Wash and sterilize the canning jars and prepare the boiling water canner and other tools. (See the canning guidelines on page 17.)

2. Combine all the ingredients in a large saucepan.

3. Bring the mixture to a boil over high heat. Allow it to boil for 5 minutes, stirring constantly.

4. Remove the saucepan from the heat. With a slotted spoon, skim off any foam on the surface of the jelly.

5. Carefully pour the jelly into the prepared jars. Process them in the boiling water canner, following the instructions on page 18.

Chokecherry Raspberry Cocktail

GF DF NF V VG — *Makes two 12-ounce drinks* — Swap: Substitute currants for chokecherries

Chokecherries and raspberries are the deep, rich, fruity base for this fizzy drink. If you grow raspberries in your garden, you are probably harvesting a late crop right around the time chokecherries are ready on the trees, so you can make the juice from your own fruit (see page 15 for instructions). If you don't grow raspberries or the fruit is out of season, you can usually find pure raspberry juice in most large supermarkets.

⅓ cup chokecherry juice (see page 15 for how to juice berries)
⅓ cup raspberry juice
3 oz gin
2 cups ginger ale
Juice of 1 lemon

Fill two tall glasses with ice. Mix the chokecherry juice, raspberry juice, and gin in a cocktail shaker. Shake to combine. Divide the mixture into the two glasses and top each with 1 cup ginger ale.

NOTE: Omit the gin for a tangy, non-alcoholic drink.

In addition to black currants (*Ribes americanum*), northern black currants (*R. hudsonianum*) and prickly currants (*R. lacustre*) are native to the prairie provinces. Red and white currants are not native to this region, so you won't find them in the wild. However, you'll have no trouble finding many cultivars of all types of currants available for purchase in nurseries and garden centres to grow in your own garden. Currants are ideal for the small space garden (or to tuck into nooks and crannies in a larger garden). They are attractive small shrubs, generally reaching a height of only 5 or 6 feet, with a similar spread. The bright green, fine-lobed leaves resemble small maple tree leaves. The leaves change to yellow or red in autumn, depending on the cultivar. Another currant of note is the clove currant (*R. aureum* var. *villosum*, sometimes listed as *R. odoratum*), which, despite the fact that it has delicious edible berries, is usually grown as an ornamental plant and features yellow flowers with an incredible spicy-sweet fragrance.

HOW TO GROW CURRANTS

Currants can tolerate some shade, although they will bear more fruit if offered full sun. Keep in mind, as well, that shadier, damp spots and dense foliage is a combination that can lead to the development of diseases such as powdery mildew.

Currants are best planted in the spring or early autumn. Don't wait too long to put them in the ground in the fall; you want to give the shrubs sufficient time to establish roots. Space individual shrubs approximately 1.5 metres apart. Unless you are creating a hedge, don't force currants to sidle up too closely to other plants; offer them a site free of competition for light, space, nutrients, and water.

Currants are not drought tolerant and will require supplemental irrigation when rainfall is insufficient during the growing season. Mulching the base of the plants with clean, weed-free straw or wood chips may help conserve moisture during hot summers and offer a bit of protection from the freeze and thaw cycles that occur on the prairies in the winter.

Currants should be given a side dressing of a 1- to 2-inch layer of compost each spring. If you choose to use a synthetic fertilizer, opt for a balanced one; high nitrogen content will spur vegetative growth but isn't likely to encourage heavy fruit production.

Don't forget to weed—and keep up with the task! It's not fun, but your currants will thank you for it (hopefully in several pounds of gorgeous berries).

Currants may sucker if their roots are disturbed through cultivation or mechanical injury—don't nick them with the weed trimmer! The suckers are easily cut away if unwanted.

Fruit production generally begins when the currants have been in the ground for at least 2 years. Fruit is usually borne on 2- and 3-year-old wood. Carefully consider this fact when you prune and don't take out the wrong branches. Plan for the future, as well, and don't trim away too much of the newer wood. Wood that is older than 3 years is generally less productive and can be removed. (It is prudent to remove no more than 25 percent of the total branches in a given growing season.) The shrubs can live up to 30 years and, with proper care, remain productive the whole time.

Currants are self-fertile, so if you only want one in your garden, go for it! It will be able to produce fruit without a pollinizer. As with many fruit-bearing plants, however, having another cultivar around may result in even more favourable yields. Insects such as bees help ensure that the transfer of pollen takes place.

PESTS AND DISEASES

The Laidback Gardener website has some great information about dealing with currant pests. Currant sawflies can do massive damage to currant plants. There are several species of this fly and, depending on where you live, you may find only certain ones. The caterpillar-like larvae can easily defoliate currant shrubs within a few days. After feeding, they drop to the ground to create a cocoon and pupate. The female adults lay eggs on the undersides of currant leaves, and when the eggs hatch, the whole feeding cycle begins anew. There could be two or three generations of currant sawflies per year—again, depending on where you live—and the larvae can overwinter in the soil. Not fun! You can hand-pick the larvae from the leaves when you see them or blast them off the foliage with water from the garden hose. If you feel comfortable using insecticidal soap, that may work as well.

Powdery mildew is a fungal disease which can severely affect currants, particularly black currants. The fungus initially causes white powdery patches on leaves and stems. The powder eventually turns brown, spreading throughout the plant. The leaves may dry up and fall off. The berries may split open. Clean up all the leaf litter at the base of the plants. Do not use fertilizer with a high nitrogen content, as this promotes tender green growth that the mildew will readily attack. As a preventative measure when planting currants, purchase cultivars that are powdery-mildew resistant.

THE NITTY GRITTY ABOUT THE FRUIT

Currant berries may be black, white, or red in colour and are borne on long, pendulous trusses commonly called strings. White currants are considered a variation of red currants—the only real difference between them is the colour of the berries.

Red and white currants should be picked when they show even colour. (They will have a shiny, transparent look to them.) Black currants do not have this clear appearance; they should be picked when they are uniformly black and showing no other hint of colour. If the berries begin to wrinkle, they are too ripe. If you plan to make jam or jelly, pick a few slightly underripe berries to throw in the mix—they have more pectin than the fully ripe ones and will help your preserves set.

Pick the fruit in clusters, removing the entire string at once. (I like to cut them off the plants with a pair of scissors.) The berries of red and white cultivars tend to be a bit more delicate than black currants, but all types should be carefully handled.

WHAT DO THEY TASTE LIKE?

Currants contain small, insignificant edible seeds that lend just a slight crunch when you bite into a berry. The berries themselves are tart, and a sweetener is generally added when they are used in cooking and baking.

CURRANT COUSINS

Currants are closely related to gooseberries, which you'll find growing
wild all over the prairies. There are also some excellent gooseberry cultivars
available for gardeners to try. Jostaberries are a cross between a black currant
and a gooseberry. Grow them in the garden in the same way you would
black currants and enjoy them in recipes such as the ones in this book!

Carrot and Currant Salad

GF DF NF V — *Serves 4 to 6 as a side dish*

Fresh garden carrots, sweet apples, and tart currants are complemented by the tangy-sweet flavours of mustard and honey. This is a delightful hang-on-to-summer salad to enjoy anytime!

3 cups grated carrots
½ cup fresh currants
1 large apple, cored, peeled, and finely chopped
3 Tbsp orange juice
2 Tbsp honey
1 tsp whole-grain mustard
Salt and pepper, to taste

1. Combine the carrots, currants, and apple in a large bowl.

2. Mix the orange juice, the honey, the mustard, and the salt and pepper in a small bowl. Add the orange juice and honey mixture to the carrots and currants and apple and mix thoroughly.

3. Keep any leftovers in the refrigerator and eat within a day.

Currant Ketchup

GF DF NF V VG — *Makes 1¾ cups of ketchup*

Fruit ketchup? you say incredulously. Why not? After all, tomatoes are a fruit, and everyone is totally okay with that. And I daresay currant ketchup is even more flavourful than any tomato ketchup I've ever eaten—sweet and hot and full of zippy berry flavour. It doesn't take that long to whip up a batch, either.

1 cup fresh currants
⅔ cup brown sugar
2 Tbsp apple cider vinegar
1 small onion, peeled and minced
1 Tbsp fresh grated ginger root

1 tsp ground mustard
½ tsp ground cinnamon
¼ tsp ground cloves
Kosher salt and ground black pepper,
  to taste

1. Place all the ingredients in a medium saucepan. Bring them to a simmer over medium-low heat. Cook for 20 minutes, or until the berries are soft and the mixture is thick. Remove the ketchup from the heat and cool to room temperature.

2. Purée the ketchup using an immersion blender or a regular blender. Add a bit of water if it is too thick. Store the ketchup in the refrigerator for up to 1 week.

Parsnip Fries to Dip in the Currant Ketchup

GF DF NF V VG — *Serves 2–4 as a side dish*

Forget potatoes! Try sweet, nutty parsnips, trimmed into sticks and baked in the oven, instead of flipped into the fryer. They are the ideal vehicle for tangy currant ketchup (see facing page).

1 lb peeled parsnips (approximately 4 medium)
1 Tbsp extra-virgin olive oil
1 garlic clove, crushed
¼ tsp kosher salt
¼ tsp ground black pepper

1. Preheat the oven to 400°F. Place a piece of parchment paper on a baking sheet.

2. Chop the parsnips into sticks (approximately 3 inches long and ½ inch thick).

3. Combine the parsnips, olive oil, garlic, salt, and pepper in a large bowl. Toss to combine, ensuring that every piece of parsnip is coated in the oil.

4. Spread the parsnip pieces on the prepared baking sheet in a single layer.

5. Bake the parsnip pieces in the preheated oven for 10 minutes. Remove the fries from the oven and, using a pair of tongs, turn them over. Return the pan to the oven and bake the fries for another 10 to 20 minutes, or until golden-crisp. Watch them carefully toward the end of their cooking time to ensure that they do not burn.

6. Remove the fries from the oven and plate them. Dip them in currant ketchup and enjoy!

Wild Rice with Currants

GF   DF   V — *Serves 4 as a side dish*

Did you know that wild rice is not a type of rice at all? It's an aquatic grass and we eat its seeds. Wild rice is actually a native plant in many regions of Canada, and there are a few specialty growers cultivating it right here on the prairies (mostly in the north, where there are larger water sources). Serve this flavourful side dish with roasted meat or poultry.

2 cups water, plus 2 Tbsp water for finishing the dish
½ cup wild rice, rinsed
¼ cup fresh currants
2 Tbsp maple syrup

2 large fresh sage leaves, minced
1½ tsp unsalted butter
¼ cup pecans, coarsely chopped

1. Bring the 2 cups of water to a boil in a large saucepan. Add the wild rice. Lower the heat, cover the pan, and cook for 1 hour, or until all the liquid is absorbed and the rice is chewy. (Check on it periodically so that it doesn't burn.) Add the currants, the maple syrup, the 2 Tbsp water, and the sage. Cook for another 10 minutes.

2. Meanwhile, in a small saucepan, melt the butter and add the pecans. Toast the pecans for 2 minutes, then remove them from the heat. Add the pecans to the wild rice and combine.

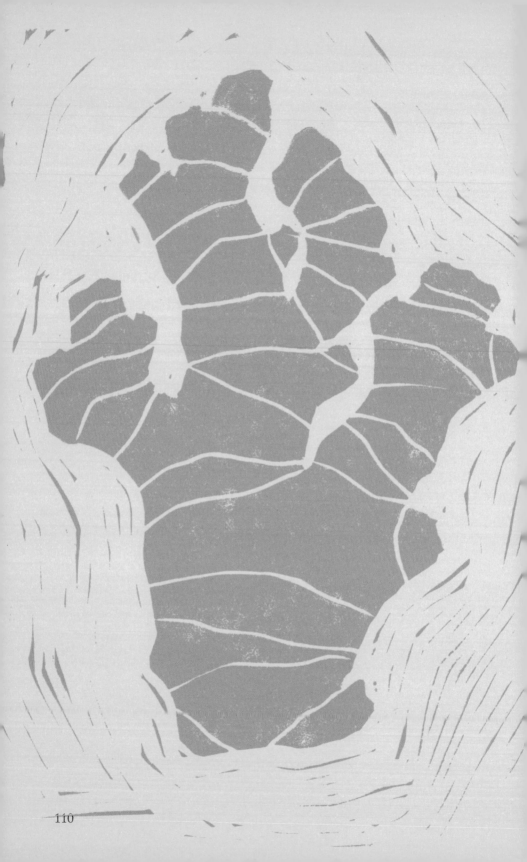

Currant Ginger Cookies

NF V — *Makes about 2 dozen cookies*

Forget raisins! These soft, full-on ginger molasses cookies positively sparkle with the addition of tangy currants.

2¼ cups all-purpose flour

1 tsp baking soda

1 tsp cornstarch

1½ tsp ground ginger

1½ tsp ground cinnamon

1 tsp ground cloves

¾ cup unsalted butter, softened

½ cup brown sugar

¼ cup granulated sugar

1 egg

⅓ cup molasses

½ cup fresh or frozen currants

1. Combine the flour, baking soda, cornstarch, ginger, cinnamon, and cloves in a medium bowl.

2. Using a stand or hand-held mixer, cream together the butter, the brown sugar, and the granulated sugar in a separate, large bowl. Add the egg and the molasses. Stir until the mixture is thoroughly combined.

3. Add the dry ingredients to the creamed mixture and stir just until combined. Fold in the currants. Do not overmix.

4. Cover the bowl with a piece of plastic wrap. Place the cookie dough in the refrigerator for approximately 2 hours to chill.

5. Preheat the oven to 350°F.

6. Line two baking sheets with parchment paper.

7. For each cookie, scoop out 2 Tbsp of cookie dough and form it into a ball. Place it on one of the baking sheets. Leave approximately 2 inches of space between each cookie ball. Repeat with the remaining cookie dough, filling the second baking sheet

8. Bake the cookies for 9 to 11 minutes, then remove them from the oven. The cookies will be very soft, so allow them to sit on the baking sheets for about 5 minutes before moving them to a wire rack to cool completely.

9. Store the cookies in an airtight container in the refrigerator for up to 1 week. They freeze very well, for up to 3 months.

Currant Meringue Cookies

GF NF DF V

Makes approx. 30 — Swap: Sour cherries, chokecherries, saskatoons, or haskap berries for currants

While meringue cookies take virtually no time to whip up (pun intended!), they need to sit in the oven afterward for several hours to properly set up. I recommend making them in the evening and letting them rest overnight. These particular meringues have a vibrant currant flavour and a pretty pink-purple hue.

2 egg whites
½ cup granulated sugar
Pinch of salt
2 Tbsp currant juice (see page 15 for how to juice berries)

1. Preheat the oven to 350°F.

2. Place a piece of parchment paper on a baking sheet.

3. Put the egg whites, sugar, and salt in a medium bowl. Using a hand-held or stand mixer on medium speed, beat the mixture for 3 minutes.

4. Add the currant juice to the egg and sugar mixture and increase the speed on the mixer to high. Beat for another 2 to 3 minutes, until the egg whites form stiff peaks and the mixture takes on a glossy appearance.

5. Pipe the meringue in small rosettes on the prepared baking sheet. (See page 65 for how to make a simple piping bag.) Use about 2 tsp of meringue for each rosette.

6. Place the cookies in the preheated oven, and immediately turn the oven off. Allow the cookies to sit in the oven for 6 to 8 hours. They will dry out and become nice and crispy, perfect for indulging that sweet tooth!

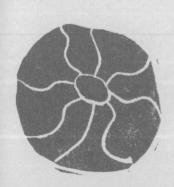

Currant and Orange Loaf

NF V — *Makes one 9 x 5-inch loaf*

If you like cranberry bread, the sweet-tart combination of currants and orange juice in this moist loaf will be a hit with you! The glaze is optional, of course, but why would you leave it out?

LOAF

2 cups all-purpose flour
¾ cup granulated sugar
1½ tsp baking powder
½ tsp baking soda
¼ cup cold unsalted butter
1 large egg, well-beaten

¾ cup orange juice
1 cup fresh or frozen currants
¾ cup white chocolate chips

GLAZE

3 Tbsp orange juice
3 tsp granulated sugar

1. Preheat the oven to 350°F.

2. Place a sheet of parchment paper into a 9- × 5-inch loaf pan, leaving an overhang on the long sides.

3. Whisk together the flour, sugar, baking powder, and baking soda in a large bowl. Cut the butter into small pieces and add it to the dry ingredients. Rub the butter into the flour mixture with your fingers. After a few minutes, the mixture should look like coarse crumbs.

4. Crack the egg into a small bowl. Whisk the egg until it is well-beaten.

5. Add the egg and the orange juice to the flour mixture and stir just until incorporated. Do not overmix. Add the currants and the white chocolate chips and mix just until combined. Spoon the batter into the prepared loaf pan.

6. Bake in the oven for 60 to 70 minutes, or until a tester inserted into the centre comes out clean.

7. Remove the loaf from the oven and lift up the overhanging ends of the parchment paper. Place the loaf on a wire rack to cool, peeling off the parchment paper.

8. Mix together the ingredients for the glaze in a small bowl. Spoon the glaze over the loaf.

9. Allow the loaf to cool completely before serving. The glaze will set as the loaf cools.

Frosted Currant Cupcakes

NF V — *Makes 12 cupcakes*

Topped with a luscious currant and buttercream frosting, these soft, fruity cupcakes are decadent enough for a party! No special occasion needed, of course . . .

CUPCAKES
1⅓ cups all-purpose flour
1 cup granulated sugar
Pinch of salt
¼ tsp baking soda
¾ tsp baking powder
½ cup low-fat milk
½ cup unsalted butter, softened
2 Tbsp currant juice (see page 15 for how to juice berries)
1 egg

FROSTING
½ cup unsalted butter, softened
3 Tbsp currant juice (see page 15 for how to juice berries)
2 cups icing sugar

1. Preheat the oven to 350°F.

2. Line a 12-cup muffin pan with parchment baking cups.

3. In a large bowl, combine the flour, sugar, salt, baking soda, baking powder, milk, and butter. Mix at low speed with a hand-held or stand mixer until smooth. Add the currant juice and the egg and combine thoroughly.

4. Divide the batter evenly between the baking cups in the muffin pan.

5. Bake for 22 minutes or until a tester inserted into the centre of one of the cupcakes comes out clean.

6. Cool the cupcakes in the pan on a wire rack.

7. To make the frosting, combine the butter, currant juice, and icing sugar in a large bowl. Beat the mixture on low speed with a hand-held or stand mixer until the icing is smooth and light.

8. Generously spread the icing on the cooled cupcakes.

9. Refrigerate any uneaten cupcakes (not that there will be any!).

Currant Butter Tarts

NF V — *Makes 6 tarts* — Swap: Sour cherries, saskatoons, or haskap berries for currants

A few years ago, in the *Toronto Sun*, Rita DeMontis wrote about the history of butter tarts. Among the interesting facts she uncovered was that the first recorded recipe for butter tarts was in a 1900 cookbook published by the Women's Auxiliary of the Royal Victoria Hospital in Barrie, Ontario. Food historians suspect that the dessert may be much older than that, however. There is speculation that the Filles du Roi (the King's Daughters), who were sent to New France between 1663 to 1673, perhaps had a similar recipe in their repertoire. We'll never know for sure, but this Canadian staple has evolved in many ways over the years, with bakers firmly entrenched regarding "extras" such as raisins, shredded coconut, or bacon (you read that correctly!). Even the consistency of the tart filling can be an issue: firm or runny. We take these things very seriously. I may have broken someone's rule by adding shredded coconut, and currant juice (instead of fruit) changes things up, but I think you'll find the results very satisfactory. And—for those who are begging to know in advance—this is a firm filling.

1 single pie crust (use half of the pie crust recipe on page 60 or your favourite pie crust)

All-purpose flour, for dusting

1 egg

¼ cup brown sugar

¼ cup corn syrup

2 Tbsp unsalted butter, melted

2 Tbsp currant juice (see page 15 for how to juice berries)

2 Tbsp unsweetened medium coconut flakes

1. Preheat the oven to 425°F.

2. Roll out the pie dough to a thickness of approximately ⅛ inch on a floured work surface. Using a butter knife or bench scraper, cut the dough into six squares.

3. Line each cup of a 6-cup muffin pan with a square of dough. Trim away the excess dough so that the cups are filled and there is no dough sticking up out of the top of each cup.

4. Whisk the egg in a small cup until well beaten.

5. In a medium bowl, combine the brown sugar, corn syrup, melted butter, currant juice, and coconut flakes. Add the egg and mix until incorporated.

6. Divide the filling mixture between the 6 pastry shells in the prepared muffin pan. Do not fill the cups more than ¾ full or you will have a very messy situation later.

7. Bake the tarts for 12 to 15 minutes, or until the filling is set and the pastry is golden brown.

8. Remove the tarts from the oven and place the muffin pan on a wire rack to cool completely. Don't try to take the tarts out of the pan while they're still warm, as the pastry may crumble. It's difficult to be patient, I know.

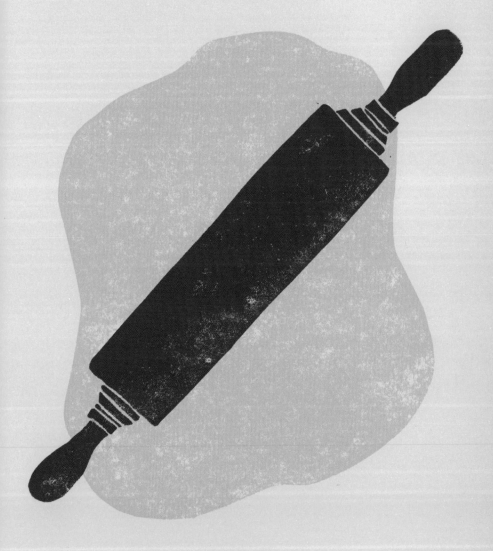

Red Currant and Almond Jelly

GF DF V — *Makes 2 quarter-pint jars*

I like the nutty finish that pure almond extract gives to this tangy-sweet jelly, but it can easily be omitted if you want to make currant jelly without any extra flavour. (If you really want to make this jelly special, add an almond flavoured liqueur such as Amaretto!) Red currants have a high pectin content, so you'll find that this recipe sets up beautifully without any added store-bought pectin—in fact, if you boil it just a little too long, you'll be hard-pressed to spread it on toast! Watch your timing. White currants may be substituted for the red, if you can't get your hands on red ones.

1 cup red currant juice (see page 15 for how to juice berries)
1 cup granulated sugar
1 Tbsp pure almond extract or Amaretto liqueur

1. Wash and sterilize the canning jars and prepare the boiling water canner and other tools as described in the canning guidelines on page 18. (Use 2 quarter-pint jars for this recipe.)

2. Combine all the ingredients in a large saucepan.

3. Bring the ingredients to a boil over high heat. Allow the mixture to boil, stirring constantly. After about 5 minutes, use a candy thermometer to see if the jelly has reached the gel point. (See page 21 for instructions on how to do that.) If the jelly has reached the correct temperature, remove it from the heat. Otherwise, keep boiling it for a few minutes longer.

4. With a slotted spoon, skim off any foam on the surface of the jelly. Carefully pour the jelly into the prepared jars. Process them in the boiling water canner, following the instructions on page 18.

Black Currant Jam

GF DF NF V VG — *Makes 3 half-pint jars*

This is some serious jam: dark, mysterious, and handsome. Well, maybe not so mysterious; it's pretty easy to make, actually. Just four ingredients and no added pectin—the way it should be.

4 cups fresh black currants, de-stemmed, washed, and dried
1½ cups granulated sugar
¼ cup orange juice
1 Tbsp fresh lemon juice

1. Follow all of the instructions on page 18 to sterilize and prepare your canning jars, screw bands, and sealing discs. (Use 3 half-pint jars for this recipe.)

2. Add all of the ingredients into a large saucepan. Stir to combine.

3. Bring the mixture to a boil over high heat, stirring frequently. Turn the heat down to medium-high and allow the mixture to continue to boil. Cook for about 15 minutes. The mixture will thicken noticeably.

4. Use a candy thermometer to take the temperature of the jam to see if it has reached the gel point. (See page 21 for more details on how to do that.) If the jam has reached the correct temperature, remove it from the heat. Otherwise, continue to boil it for a few more minutes. Pour the jam into the prepared jars, and process it according to the instructions on page 18.

Currant Lemon Rum Sour

GF DF NF V VG — *Makes 2 approximately 12-ounce drinks*

Traditional rum sours usually contain egg whites but we're forgoing that . . . well, we're adding currant juice and sparkling water, so it's not really a rum sour at all. Except that it has rum in it and it's sour. Let's not think too hard about it and drink up instead!

3 oz spiced rum
¼ cup currant juice (see page 15 for how to juice berries)
¼ cup fresh lemon juice
¼ cup simple syrup (see page 73 for how to make simple syrup)
Crushed ice
¾ cup sparkling water or ginger ale, divided
Lemon slices, as garnish

Put the rum, currant juice, lemon juice, and simple sugar in a cocktail shaker. Shake well. Divide the mixture between two tall glasses containing crushed ice. Top with the sparkling water or ginger ale and garnish with lemon slices.

SEA

BUCKTHORN

Common sea buckthorn (*Hippophae rhamnoides*) is native to salty seashores and riverbanks in a many parts of Europe and Asia, but this tough-as-nails, cold hardy (to zone 3) shrub also performs well in the hot, dry, and open spaces of the Canadian prairies. Sea buckthorn is often used in this arid, cold climate to prevent soil erosion from high winds and as a natural snow fence.

In his book *Grow Fruit Naturally: A Hands-On Guide to Luscious, Home-Grown Fruit*, Lee Reich acknowledges the dual nature of sea buckthorn. The shrub is truly a mix of beauty and beast: formidable 2-inch thorns tip the stems on many cultivars, while the female plants bear gorgeous clusters of small orange berries in autumn. (Sea buckthorn are dioecious, and male and female plants must be grown together for fruit production to occur. One male plant can pollinate up to seven females.) The berries are persistent on the plants, which means that they do not produce much in the way of fruit litter, and the berries that are not harvested or eaten by birds look absolutely incredible against the white snows of winter.

Sea buckthorn is a large shrub, reaching up to 20 feet tall, with a similar spread in our climate. The thin, lance-like leaves are an attractive silver-green in colour and are borne on brown, scaly (and did I mention poky?) stems. Yellow flowers appear in early spring and are so insignificant and short-lived that you might miss them if you blink. Fortunately, they are followed a few months later by the showstopping, densely clustered berries.

Despite the fact that they are not legumes, sea buckthorns are nitrogen fixing plants. They have a symbiotic relationship with a special bacteria (from the genus *Frankia*), which will take nitrogen from the air and convert it to a form that the plants can consume. As a result, sea buckthorns usually do not require applications of a nitrogen-based fertilizer.

Sea buckthorn is highly tolerant of both wet and dry conditions. Its ability to withstand drought means that it can serve beautifully as a xeriscape specimen. As befitting a plant that can grow along the seashore, sea buckthorn is well-suited to the saline soils that may be found in prairie landscapes. It is adaptable to a wide range of soil types but requires excellent drainage for success.

One major thing to note before you rush out to purchase sea buckthorn shrubs for your yard: they have an extensive rhizomatous root system, which means that they produce suckers with a flourish—and I am actually understating that! They must be properly sited so that this propensity isn't a problem for the gardener. Try these aggressive spreaders in mass plantings as shelterbelt specimens, hedging material, or in an orchard.

Sea buckthorns love to bask in the sunlight—don't park them in the shade or you won't get the berries you need to make all these delicious recipes.

Sea buckthorns do not need regular pruning. If you need to remove a crossed or dead branch, undertake the task right after the shrub flowers in the spring. As berries are produced on 2-year-old wood, it is prudent to only remove older stems.

PESTS AND DISEASES

Sea buckthorn is largely pest-free; no one wants to tangle with it. The thorns place sea buckthorn shrubs firmly on the deer resistant plant list, but birds don't seem to mind and may nest in the safety of the branches. Mice and voles will sometimes girdle the stems, especially during the winter. Wire mesh tree guards may be sunk into the soil around the shrubs to protect them from rodents.

WHEN CAN I EAT SEA BUCKTHORN BERRIES?

Once established in the ground, female sea buckthorn plants usually take 2 full growing seasons before they bear fruit. (If you're growing them from seed, count on 4 years.) Sea buckthorn berries are usually harvested in September on the Canadian prairies. If left on the shrubs, the berries won't fall off but rather become overripe and give off a cloying, fermented odour. They are not good to eat at that stage. It is suggested that a light frost improves the flavour of the fruit—and, actually, the fruit is much easier to remove from the branches if it is frozen first. (Growers sometimes wait until the branches freeze, then do a creative prune, removing the entire limb to take off the berries. I wouldn't necessarily recommend this for home gardeners. Consider that fruit production is done on second-year wood so if you take those branches away, you will have significantly reduced yields the next year.)

There are actually some thornless varieties available on the market now, which, come harvest time, should make things easier for the gardener!

WHAT DO SEA BUCKTHORN BERRIES TASTE LIKE?

Although nicknamed "Russian pineapple," sea buckthorn berries tend to be more tart than sweet when eaten fresh, but the citrusy zing when you pop one in your mouth is irresistible. They contain multiple small, extremely hard (but fully edible) seeds. Sea buckthorn berry juice, purée, or dried berries are often used in recipes rather than whole fresh berries. Sea buckthorn leaves are also edible. The leaves from male plants can be harvested in the spring, leaving the female plants to focus on fruit production later in the season.

Sea Buckthorn Berry and Butternut Squash Soup

GF DF NF — *Makes 4 servings for a lunch or dinner entrée*

Although winter squash is available in the grocery store year-round, I think of the various types as autumn staples—and, indeed, if you're growing them in your garden, you'll be harvesting them right around the time the sea buckthorn berries are ready to pick. If you didn't plant butternut squash, pumpkins will work perfectly in this recipe. (If it is a large pumpkin, you'll need to cut it up to roast it.) This is a warm, inviting soup, ideal for cooler days. Serve it with sourdough bread hot out of the oven and herb butter.

5 to 6 cups butternut squash

1 Tbsp extra-virgin olive oil

1 small onion, finely chopped

2 garlic cloves, crushed

1 Tbsp fresh gingerroot, grated

1 celery stalk, finely chopped

2¾ cups chicken stock

¼ cup sea buckthorn berry juice (see page 15 for how to juice berries)

Kosher salt and ground black pepper, to taste

1. First, roast the butternut squash. Preheat the oven to 425°F. Place a piece of parchment paper on a baking sheet. Pierce the skin of the butternut squash in several places with a fork. Place the squash on the baking sheet and bake in the oven for 60 minutes.

2. Remove the squash from the oven and allow it to cool to room temperature. To use it in this recipe, cut the roasted squash in half lengthwise and scoop out the seeds, discarding them. Scrape out the flesh of the squash and measure it for the soup.

3. In a large saucepan, heat the olive oil over medium heat. Add the onion and cook until it is softened, about 5 minutes. Add the garlic and ginger root and cook for 1 minute. Add the celery, butternut squash, chicken stock, and sea buckthorn juice. Bring the mixture to a boil, then turn the heat down to medium-low. Simmer the soup, uncovered, for 15 minutes, stirring frequently.

4. Remove the soup from the heat and serve.

Couscous Vegetable Salad with Sea Buckthorn Berry Dressing

DF NF V VG — *Serves 4 as a side dish*

This fresh, flavourful salad is a cinch to make and is ideal for taking to a potluck or tucking into a work or school lunch. If you have to eat gluten free, there is a couscous doppelgänger on the market that is made from corn, so you don't have to miss out—and, as a bonus, it cooks up just as quickly as the wheat! If you don't like couscous, bulgur or millet would work just as well, although the cooking time will increase.

1 cup water

1 cup couscous

4 green onions, chopped

12 cherry or grape tomatoes, halved

1 cup cucumber, chopped

1 cup fresh parsley, chopped

¼ cup extra-virgin olive oil

¼ cup sea buckthorn berry juice (see page 15 for how to juice berries)

Kosher salt and ground black pepper, to taste

1. Bring the water to a boil in a medium saucepan. Add the couscous and stir. Remove the couscous from the heat and put the lid on the pan. Allow the couscous to sit 5 minutes or until the water is completely absorbed. Fluff the couscous with a fork. Place the couscous in a large bowl and put it in the refrigerator.

2. Once the couscous is cooled, add the green onions, the tomatoes, the cucumber, and the parsley to the bowl and combine them with the couscous.

3. In a separate small bowl, whisk together the olive oil, the sea buckthorn berry juice, and the salt and pepper. Add the dressing to the couscous and vegetables, mix thoroughly.

Pan-Fried Salmon with Sea Buckthorn Berry Sauce

NF — *Makes 2 servings*

The citrusy zip of sea buckthorn and herbs are an ideal complement to a pan-fried salmon fillet for a quick and easy suppertime dish. Serve this alongside hot basmati or jasmine rice and steamed garden-fresh peas and carrots. A char species such as brook trout is an excellent substitute for the salmon.

SALMON

1 tsp kosher salt

1 tsp ground black pepper

⅓ cup all-purpose flour

1 large salmon fillet

2 Tbsp unsalted butter

3 Tbsp extra-virgin olive oil

SAUCE

½ cup sea buckthorn berry juice (see page 15 for how to juice berries)

3 Tbsp fresh lemon juice

2 tsp fresh basil, minced

2 tsp fresh thyme, minced

¼ cup fresh chives, chopped

1. Mix the salt, pepper, and flour on a large plate. Dredge the fresh salmon fillet in the flour mixture until it is coated on both sides. Dispose of the excess flour mixture.

2. Place a large skillet over medium heat and melt the butter. Add the olive oil.

3. Add the salmon fillet to the skillet and fry it until it is golden brown, about 4 minutes. Turn it over and fry it for about 3 to 4 minutes longer or until the underside of the salmon looks firm.

4. In the meantime, prepare the sauce. Combine all of the sauce ingredients except for the chives in a medium saucepan and heat on medium-low heat just until it reaches the boiling point. Remove the sauce from the heat.

5. Plate the salmon fillet and pour the sauce over it. Sprinkle the fresh chopped chives on the salmon.

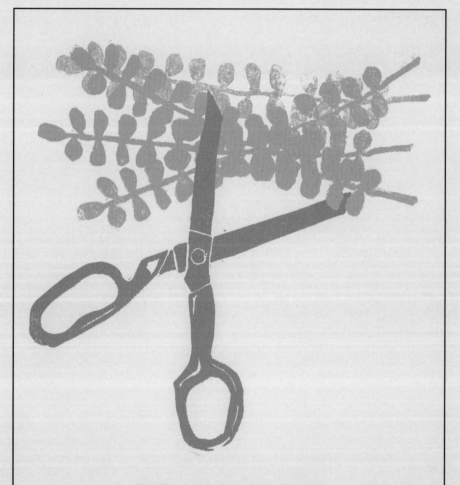

HOW TO FINELY CUT HERBS

Use a pair of kitchen scissors (or herb scissors if you have them), not a knife, to cut fresh herbs into small pieces. By using scissors, you have way more control and can cut herbs more precisely into thin or thick chiffonade strips.

Shrimp with Sea Buckthorn Berry Sauce

DF NF — *Serves 4 as a dinner entrée*

Put a tablecloth on the table, light some candles, and break out a nice bottle of wine. This is a deceptively fancy restaurant-style meal that you can make in a few minutes at home. These delectable shrimp are excellent with hot basmati rice and fresh steamed snap peas, red peppers, and green beans.

SHRIMP

20 raw jumbo shrimp, peeled and deveined

1 Tbsp toasted sesame oil

1 Tbsp vegetable oil

SAUCE

⅓ cup sea buckthorn berry juice
   (see page 15 for how to juice berries)

⅓ cup chicken broth

2 Tbsp soy sauce

2 tsp granulated sugar

2 tsp cornstarch

1 Tbsp minced garlic

1 Tbsp minced fresh ginger root

2 green onions, chopped

Kosher salt and pepper, to taste

1. Place the shrimp in a large plastic zippered bag. Add the toasted sesame oil. Seal the bag and shake it until the shrimp is completely coated in the oil.

2. Heat the vegetable oil in a large skillet over medium heat. Add the shrimp and cook until they are pink, turning frequently with a pair of tongs. Remove the shrimp from the heat and put on a plate.

3. Combine all the sauce ingredients in a medium bowl and add the sauce to the skillet that you cooked the shrimp in. Return the pan to the heat and cook until the sauce bubbles and thickens, about 2 to 3 minutes.

4. Add the shrimp to the pan and mix them with the sauce. Warm them one minute, then plate them for serving.

Chicken Fingers with Sea Buckthorn Berry Sauce

DF NF — *Makes approximately 12 chicken fingers and ½ cup of sauce*

I'm always hearing how chicken fingers are just for children—let's bust that myth! First of all, don't buy premade chicken fingers. Make them yourself. They are fast and easy to prepare, and once you've done it, you'll never go back to store-bought. Secondly, make a sophisticated dip, such as one that contains sea buckthorn berry juice. Kids and adults alike will love these—make a double batch!

SEA BUCKTHORN BERRY SAUCE
- ½ cup sea buckthorn berry juice (see page 15 for how to juice berries)
- 2 Tbsp apple cider vinegar
- 1 Tbsp granulated sugar
- ½ tsp soy sauce
- ½ tsp ground mustard
- 2 garlic cloves, minced
- Pinch of kosher salt
- 2 Tbsp water
- 2 tsp cornstarch

CHICKEN FINGERS
- 2 skinless, boneless chicken breasts
- ½ cup all-purpose flour
- ¼ tsp kosher salt
- Pinch of ground black pepper
- ½ cup vegetable oil for frying, divided

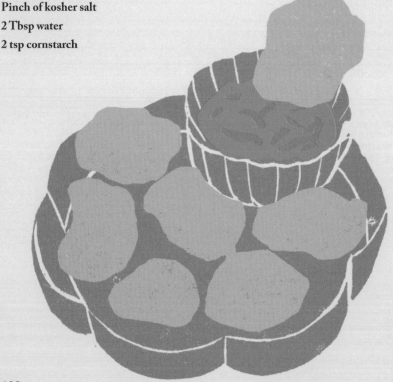

1. First make the sea buckthorn berry sauce. In a small saucepan, mix together the sea buckthorn berry juice, the apple cider vinegar, the sugar, the soy sauce, the mustard, the garlic, and the salt. Bring to a simmer over medium-low heat and cook for 5 minutes.

2. Blend the water and cornstarch in a small cup. Drizzle the cornstarch mixture into the sauce and stir. Cook for another 2 minutes. The mixture will thicken.

3. Remove the sauce from the heat and allow it to cool to room temperature. Place it in the refrigerator for at least 1 hour before serving it with the chicken fingers.

4. To make the chicken fingers, cut the chicken into 12 strips. (Each strip should be approximately ½ inch wide and 2 inches long.)

5. Mix the flour, salt, and pepper on a large plate. Roll the chicken pieces in the flour mixture to coat them.

6. Pour ¼ cup of the vegetable oil into a large skillet and heat it over medium heat. Add 6 of the chicken fingers to the hot oil. Fry for 3 minutes on each side or until golden-brown and crisp. Remove the chicken fingers from the pan and put them on a piece of paper towel to catch any excess oil.

7. Add the rest of the oil to the skillet and fry the final batch of chicken fingers.

8. Serve the chicken fingers with the sea buckthorn berry sauce.

Sea Buckthorn Berry Frozen Dessert

GF V — *Serves 4 for dessert*

This cold, citrusy treat is better than a popsicle any day! The preparation is quick and easy, but the dessert takes several hours to freeze, so plan ahead.

1 cup sea buckthorn berry juice (see page 15 for how to juice berries)
⅔ cup sweetened condensed milk
Pinch of kosher salt
1 cup whipping cream (35%)
2 Tbsp crushed pistachios

1. In a large bowl, mix the sea buckthorn berry juice, sweetened condensed milk, and salt.

2. In a medium bowl, whip the cream to stiff peaks with a hand-held or stand mixer.

3. Fold the whipping cream into the sea buckthorn berry and condensed milk mixture. Stir in the pistachios.

4. Cover the bowl with plastic wrap and put the dessert into the freezer. Freeze it for 6 hours.

5. Allow the mixture to sit at room temperature for about 5 minutes before serving.

Sea Buckthorn Berry Custard

GF NF V — *Makes 1 cup of custard*

In the past, I have made sea buckthorn berry custard with eggs, but this way is far quicker and doesn't involve separating egg yolks from whites. (Plus, if you or someone you are cooking for has an allergy to eggs, this recipe is safe to eat.) You can slather this custard between layers of a white cake, use it to fill cookies (see page 143), or—and I admit this is my favourite thing to do with it—shamelessly eat it out of the pan. No, it's not a true custard, but it sure acts like one.

⅓ cup sea buckthorn berry juice (see page 15 for how to juice berries)
¼ cup unsalted butter
¼ cup granulated sugar
2 Tbsp sweetened condensed milk
2 Tbsp cornstarch
1 Tbsp cold water

1. Combine the sea buckthorn berry juice, the butter, the sugar, and the sweetened condensed milk in a small saucepan. Warm the mixture over medium-low heat and simmer for 5 minutes, stirring frequently.

2. In the meantime, combine the cornstarch and the water in a small cup. Drizzle the cornstarch mixture into the sea buckthorn berry juice and sugar mixture and stir until thickened, 1 to 2 minutes. Remove the custard from the heat.

3. Cool the custard to room temperature before spooning it into an airtight container and placing it in the refrigerator for up to 2 hours.

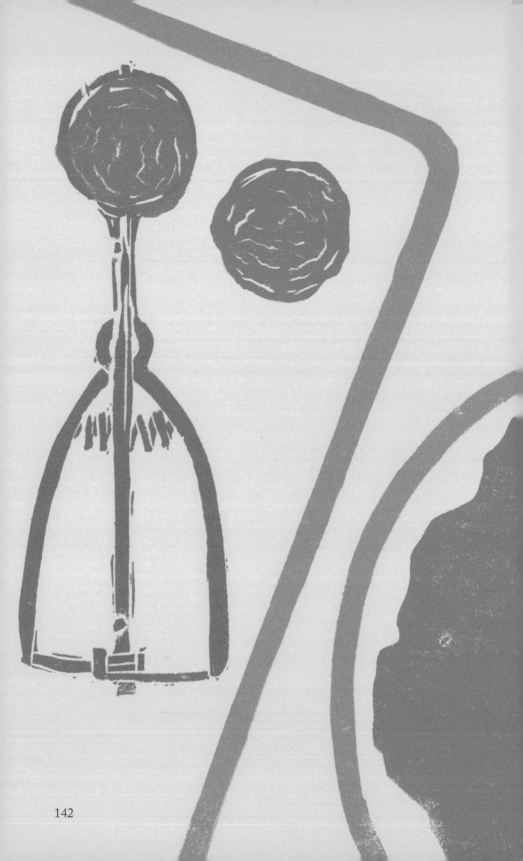

Thumbprint Cookies with Sea Buckthorn Berry Custard

NF V — *Makes about 15 cookies*

This light, flaky, buttery cookie is scrumptiously filled with sea buckthorn berry custard (see page 141). If you've made the haskap, currant, saskatoon, or chokecherry jam and jelly recipes in this book, you could use them to fill the cookies instead of the custard. Or as well. I'm firmly in the "as well" camp.

1 cup all-purpose flour
½ cup cold unsalted butter, cut into small pieces
3 Tbsp sweetened condensed milk
3 Tbsp sea buckthorn custard, divided (see page 141)

1. Preheat the oven to 350°F.

2. Line a baking sheet with parchment paper.

3. Combine the flour, the butter, and the sweetened condensed milk in a large bowl and whip them together with a hand-held or stand mixer until a soft dough forms.

4. Using a 1 Tbsp cookie scoop, scoop the dough and roll into balls and place them on the prepared baking sheet. Press the top of each cookie with the tip of your thumb, making an indentation in the centre.

5. Bake the cookies for 12 to 15 minutes. Do not overbake. These should just barely take on a golden hue at the bottom of each cookie. Remove them from the oven.

6. Wait 5 minutes until the cookies firm up, then take them off the baking sheet and set on a wire rack to cool.

7. Fill the indentation in each cookie with a small dab of the sea buckthorn custard. Wait until the cookies are completely cooled before eating—these taste better when they are not warm.

Sea Buckthorn Berry Oatmeal Cookies

NF V — *Makes about 2 dozen cookies*

There are a bazillion oatmeal cookie recipes out there, but I'll bet you've never found one that contains sea buckthorn berry juice . . . until now. This is an adaptation of the deliciously coconutty oatmeal cookie recipe that has been a staple in my kitchen for years, and now that I've tried it with sea buckthorn berries, there is no going back. These cookies firm up a few minutes after they've been removed from the oven, so let them sit on the baking sheet briefly before taking them off and putting them on wire racks to cool completely.

½ cup butter, softened

½ cup granulated sugar

½ cup brown sugar

1 egg

2 Tbsp sea buckthorn berry juice (see page 15 for how to juice berries)

½ cup plus 2 Tbsp all-purpose flour

¼ tsp baking soda

1 cup unsweetened shredded coconut

1½ cups quick oats

1. Preheat the oven to 350°F.

2. Line two baking sheets with parchment paper.

3. In a large bowl, with a hand-held or stand mixer, cream the butter and sugars. Add the egg and the sea buckthorn berry juice.

4. In a small bowl, combine the flour and the baking soda. Add it to the creamed butter and sugar mixture.

5. Fold in the coconut and the quick oats.

6. Roll the cookie dough into 1-inch balls. Place them on the prepared baking sheets.

7. Bake the cookies for 8 to 10 minutes. Don't allow them to overbake and get too dark in colour. Let the cookies cool on the baking sheets before transferring them to a wire rack to cool completely.

Sea Buckthorn Berry Blondies

NF V — *Makes one 8-inch pan of brownies*

Although I am a devoted fan of chocolate brownies, I think I adore blondies (also known as butterscotch brownies) even more. In this case, I went all out with the friendly flavours of sea buckthorn berry juice, butterscotch, and white chocolate. If you have to make a special treat to take to a work luncheon or a meeting, these should be your go-tos—and, as a bonus, they are a quick bar cookie to whip up when you have a zillion other things to do.

1¼ cups all-purpose flour
¼ tsp kosher salt
½ cup unsalted butter, softened
1½ cups brown sugar

2 eggs
1 Tbsp sea buckthorn berry juice (see page 15 for how to juice berries)
¼ cup white chocolate chips

1. Preheat the oven to 350°F.

2. Place a piece of parchment paper in an 8-inch square cake pan.

3. Blend together the flour and salt in a small bowl.

4. Using a hand-held or stand mixer, beat the butter and the brown sugar in a large bowl until light and fluffy. Add the eggs and the sea buckthorn berry juice and mix.

5. Add the flour mixture to the wet ingredients and stir to combine. Fold in the chocolate chips.

6. Turn the batter into the prepared pan.

7. Bake the blondies for 25 to 30 minutes, or until a tester inserted into the centre of the blondies comes out clean.

8. Cool the pan of blondies thoroughly on a wire rack before cutting it into bars.

Sea Buckthorn Berry and Mango Salsa

GF DF NF V VG — *Makes 2 cups of salsa*

Fresh and freakishly addictive. This is one of those ideal snacks for a late-summer afternoon on the patio. Serve with lightly salted corn chips or crackers.

2 mangoes, peeled, pitted, and chopped finely
1 jalapeño pepper, deseeded and minced
1 large tomato, chopped finely
¼ cup finely chopped fresh cilantro leaves
2 green onions, chopped finely
¼ cup sea buckthorn berry juice (see page 15 for how to juice berries)
1 Tbsp fresh lime juice
Kosher salt and ground black pepper, to taste

Combine all of the ingredients in a large bowl and serve.

Sea Buckthorn Berry and Apple Jelly

GF DF NF V VG — *Makes 2 half-pint jars*

Back in 2012, when I posted an early version of this recipe on my blog *Flowery Prose*, I never anticipated that it would turn out to be one of my most popular posts ever, but every year, during harvest time in late summer and early autumn, the hits just keep coming! And there is good reason: The combination of sea buckthorn berries and apples is irresistible, and the colour of this jelly is spectacular. As a bonus, the apples have a high pectin content, so there is no need to add commercial pectin to this beautiful and flavourful jelly.

4 cups fresh or frozen sea buckthorn
   berries, washed thoroughly

3 apples, washed, peeled, cored, and diced
   finely (if you don't want to go to the
   trouble, and your apples are organic,
   you can leave the peels on)

½ cup water

2 cups granulated sugar

1. Place the sea buckthorn berries, the diced apples, and the water in a saucepan and bring to a boil. Reduce the heat to medium-low and simmer the fruit for 20 minutes. Stir periodically and crush the fruit against the side of the pan with the back of a spoon. (It all mashes down pretty well on its own and won't require much additional help.)

2. Strain the fruit through a jelly bag (or several layers of cheesecloth) over a large bowl. Don't force the fruit through the bag—this will make the jelly cloudy, and you don't want that! Set it up so that the fruit can slowly strain overnight.

3. In the morning, sterilize your canning jars, sealing discs, and screw bands following the instructions on page 18.

4. Measure out 2 cups of the juice. Place the juice into a saucepan and add the sugar. Bring the sugar and juice to a rolling boil and hold it at that heat, stirring constantly. After approximately 5 minutes, use a candy thermometer to see if the jelly has reached the gel point. (See page 21 for further tips about this stage.) If the jelly has reached the correct temperature, remove it from the heat. Otherwise, continue to boil the jelly for a few more minutes.

5. Fill the jars with the jelly and process them in a boiling water canner. (See page 18 for guidelines on water bath canning.)

Sea Buckthorn Berry and
Earl Grey Tea Cocktail

GF   DF   NF   V   VG — *Makes two 12-ounce drinks*

I'm a huge fan of the flavour of Earl Grey tea—there is something really warm and appealing about the bergamot (which, contrary to commonly held belief, is actually from the oil of a citrus fruit and not the herb from the genus *Monarda*, even though the fragrance is similar). This cocktail is all about the unique orange-flavoured combination of the bergamot and the sea buckthorn berry juice. Well, and the gin too! Can't forget that.

Ice cubes
6 oz gin
½ cup sea buckthorn berry juice (see page 15 for how to juice berries)
2 ½ cups Earl Grey tea, steeped and chilled (made from 1 Earl Grey teabag)
2 tsp granulated sugar

Fill two tall glasses with the ice. Place the gin, the sea buckthorn berry juice, the tea, and the sugar into a cocktail shaker and mix. Divide the mixture between the two glasses and serve.

NOTE: Omit the gin for a citrusy, non-alcoholic drink. This one is particularly refreshing at breakfast time!

SOUR
CHERRIES

In the cultivation manual *Dwarf Sour Cherries: A Guide for Commercial Production*, Bob Bors and Linda Matthews note that the intercrossing of European tart cherries (*Prunus cerasus*) and Mongolian cherries (*P. fruticosa*) has resulted in the creation of several diminutive sour cherry trees (*P. x kerrasis*)—perfect for small yards! In addition to their desirable size and delicious fruit, many cultivars of dwarf sour cherries are hardy to zone 3, which makes them perfect candidates for prairie edible gardens.

There are several cultivars of dwarf sour cherries, most developed at the University of Saskatchewan. They range in size from 5 to 8 feet tall, some multi-stemmed. Dwarf sour cherries are not grafted, which means you don't have to worry about malformed graft unions or trees becoming dominated by their rootstocks. Another boon for the small-space gardener: Dwarf sour cherries are self-fertile, and, therefore, only 1 tree is required to produce fruit. There is no need to worry about obtaining the appropriate pollinizers. Bees are the primary pollinators, and you'll spot many of them when the flowers are in bloom! One thing to remember before purchasing dwarf sour cherries: while they don't produce root suckers as much as Mongolian cherries, they may do so periodically, especially if injured or if the soil nearby is disturbed. The suckers can be easily topped if unwanted.

SITING AND PLANTING DWARF SOUR CHERRIES

Sour cherries are adaptable to soil with good drainage. Side-dressing the trees with a few handfuls of compost every spring will provide sufficient nutrients for the growing season.

Full sun is best for maximum fruit production. Offer dwarf sour cherries approximately 7 feet of space separating them from other nearby trees. This will allow for proper air circulation.

Sour cherry trees are frequently purchased from the nursery in containers. Plant them as soon as you can in the spring or the early autumn. (Summertime temperatures can sometimes be too hot and send a tree spiralling into transplant shock. Likewise, don't wait too close to the onset of winter, as the tree roots will need time to establish before being subjected to ice and frozen temperatures.)

The hole you dig should be large enough to encompass the whole root ball of the tree. Sink the tree into the ground a bit deeper than it was in the pot, about 1 to 2 inches. No fertilizer is necessary at planting time. Give the newly planted tree a good soaking of water at the time of planting, and maintain a regular watering schedule thereafter.

Like other fruit trees, sour cherry trees are not tolerant of encroaching weeds or turf grass, so keep up with these cultivation tasks to keep the trees happy. Mulching the base of the trees with dry leaves, grass clippings, or weed-free straw will help prevent weed growth, conserve moisture, and cushion against freeze and thaw cycles during the prairie winter.

Periodically prune dwarf sour cherry trees to thin the branches and make it easier to pick the fruit. Don't cut more than 25 percent of the canopy away in a growing season, as it will reduce fruit yield the following year. Pruning should take place in early spring before the tree breaks dormancy. Pruning in the summer or the fall may spur the tree to produce growth late in the year and cause it to be unprepared for winter dormancy. However, pruning of diseased or damaged branches can take place at any time.

POTENTIAL PROBLEMS

According to "Dwarf Sour Cherries for the Prairies," a very informative document written by Bob Bors and Rick Sawatzky at the University of Saskatchewan, deer, rabbits, and voles are common wildlife pests of sour cherry trees, particularly in the winter, when they munch on the barks of trees and potentially cause girdling. Erecting a wire tree guard that is tall enough to prevent deer and rabbits from chowing down and that is sunk several inches into the ground so that voles cannot dig beneath it is an excellent preventative measure. Deer may still chew on the branches if they are hungry enough, however, and deterring them from doing so may require other measures, such as building a deer-proof fence around the garden or trying repellent products made from particularly smelly ingredients such as garlic, eggs, meat proteins, and predator urine.

Birds may get to the fruit before you manage to harvest it. Netting trees can be a difficult task, and it may be unappealing from an aesthetic perspective. Try noisemakers such as wind chimes and visual deterrents such as whirligigs or reflective tape hung in strips. You'll have to move these objects every few days so that the birds do not get used to them.

Split fruit is a result of inconsistent applications of water while the cherries are ripening. This may not be due to any oversight on your part, though—hot, dry weather followed by heavy, prolonged rains can cause splitting. If you need to water due to drought during this time, adhere to a regular watering schedule and apply consistent amounts of H_2O.

There are a few different types of leaf spots which may affect dwarf sour cherries. They are unsightly but usually won't significantly damage the tree. The leaves may exhibit spotting, turn yellow, and prematurely drop off. Ensure the leaf litter beneath the trees is cleaned up. (Do not put it in the compost.) Do not water up into the leaves of the tree; keep irrigation water to the base of the plant to discourage the spread of fungal spores.

LET'S TALK ABOUT WHY WE'RE ALL HERE: THE FRUIT!

Showy clusters of white flowers make a massive statement in late May—a perfect harbinger of spring. (The only problem is if we get a late frost and the blossoms are destroyed, hindering fruit production for the year.) The oval, serrated leaves are dark green and glossy, attractive in their own right. But the fruit is what we're all really waiting for. Dwarf sour cherries will start to produce fruit approximately 3 growing seasons after they have been planted. (This depends on the size of the plants when they were put into the ground.)

In early to mid-August, sour cherries begin to ripen on the trees. It is tempting to pick them the second you see a flash of red colour, but you need to wait patiently until the fruit reaches the colour it is supposed to be when ready. Some cultivars are darker red than others, almost a red-black, while others are more of a candy apple hue. Picking them too soon will yield a hard, dry fruit. The cherries should give just a little when the skin is pressed—if your finger goes through the fruit and hits the pit, you've waited too long to pick. The fruit is too ripe. You can do a taste test to see if the fruit is ready, but the success of this approach is predicated on knowing what the cherries should taste like. Fully ripe cherries are sweeter than those that are not quite ripe, so wait until the right time to pick them. If you have the space to do so, one way to increase the length of the harvest is to plant several different cultivars of dwarf sour cherries from both the early and late-season categories.

Hand-picking sour cherries is the best way to minimize damage to the fruit. Leaving the stems on the fruit will bolster the length of time the fruit can be stored fresh. (If the stems are removed at this stage, they may tear the fruit and invite decay.) As with any berries or fruit, it is best to harvest in the cool of the morning, as midday heat can cause the fruit to rapidly spoil.

Sour cherries, like sweet cherries, have a large, hard, round pit inside the fruit. You don't want to eat this, as the seeds contain amygdalin, a naturally occurring cyanogenic glycoside, which can break down into cyanide when ingested. You also don't want to accidentally bite down on one when eating something made from cherries—your dentist may be happy with the paycheque, though!

The fruit must be pitted before consumption. To do this, use a chopstick as an inexpensive, efficient tool. Press the narrow tip of the chopstick against the stem end of the cherry and press firmly. The pit will pop out the blossom side and can be discarded. If you have hundreds of cherries to pit, doing each one manually can be a chore (although you can really get a rhythm going if you put on a good movie and pit while watching). Store-bought cherry pitters can pit multiple fruits at once—but, if you decide to purchase one, bear in mind that sour cherries tend to have smaller fruit than the sweet cherries the machines were designed for. Check to ensure that the pitter you buy will be suitable.

WHAT DO SOUR CHERRIES TASTE LIKE?

As for the flavour—yes, they are a little more sour than the sweet cherries you purchase from British Columbia or Washington State, but they actually have a high sugar content and are satisfying to most palates when eaten fresh.

Sour Cherry and Zucchini Muffins

NF V — *Makes 16 large muffins*

Every year in midsummer, those of us who grow zucchini find ourselves with a bit too much of a good thing. It doesn't matter if you're growing 1 plant or 20, zucchini plants usually outdo themselves to produce a copious bounty of fruit, and, at some point, you (and your neighbours) will be swimming in this versatile summer squash. Fortunately, sour cherries are ready around the same time, and you can make several batches of this recipe to freeze for days when the zucchini harvest is but a dream. (Honestly, those days are real!)

2 large eggs
1⅓ cups granulated sugar
1 tsp almond extract
¾ cup unsalted butter, melted
2 cups fresh grated zucchini
2¾ cups all-purpose flour

1 tsp baking soda
1 tsp baking powder
1 tsp ground ginger
¼ tsp kosher salt
1½ cups fresh or frozen sour cherries

1. Preheat the oven to 350°F.

2. Line a muffin tin with parchment paper cups.

3. In a large bowl, mix the eggs, sugar, and almond extract. Add the butter and the zucchini and combine.

4. In a separate medium bowl, mix the flour, baking soda, baking powder, ginger, and salt.

5. Add the dry ingredients to the wet ingredients and mix just until combined. Fold in the sour cherries.

6. Spoon the batter into the muffin cups, dividing the mixture evenly and filling the cups about ¾ full.

7. Bake the muffins in the preheated oven for 20 to 30 minutes, or until a tester inserted in the middle of a muffin comes out clean.

8. Remove the muffins from the oven. Cool them in the pan on a wire rack.

Sour Cherry and Date Bread

V — *Makes one 9- × 5-inch loaf*

This "quick" bread takes a long time to make. A sizeable chunk out of an evening, in fact—but it's so unbelievably delicious that you'll never regret making it. (Plus, most of it is baking time, so you can chillax and stream a good movie while the bread is in the oven.)

2 cups chopped dates

1 cup boiling water

¼ cup plus 2 Tbsp unsalted butter, softened

1 egg

2 cups all-purpose flour

¾ cup granulated sugar

2 Tbsp ground flaxseed

1 tsp baking powder

⅛ tsp kosher salt

1½ cups fresh or frozen sour cherries

½ cup coarsely chopped pecans

1. Preheat the oven to 325°F.

2. Line a 9- × 5-inch loaf pan with a piece of parchment paper.

3. In a large bowl, mix the dates, the boiling water, and the butter. Set the bowl aside for 30 minutes. The dates will plump up and absorb some of the water. Add the egg to the date and butter mixture and stir to combine.

4. In a separate medium bowl, mix the flour, sugar, flaxseed, baking powder, and salt.

5. Add the flour mixture to the date and butter mixture and stir. Fold in the cherries and the pecans.

6. Spoon the batter into the prepared loaf pan. Bake the bread in the oven for 1 hour and 15 minutes, or until a tester inserted in the centre comes out clean.

7. Remove the bread from the oven. Let it sit in the pan for 10 minutes, then remove it from the pan and allow it to cool completely on a wire rack.

Sweet Potato and Sour Cherry Curry

GF DF NF V VG — *Makes approximately 4 servings for a lunch or dinner entrée*

This mild, meatless curry is characterized by the melding of the fragrant garam masala and the fruity sour cherries, resulting in a sweet, unique flavour. You can step things up in the spice department by adding more red pepper flakes or by spooning in some curry paste. Don't be surprised when the cherries break down into juice during cooking—you will still get their full-on fruity flavour.

1 Tbsp extra-virgin olive oil

1 small onion, chopped

2 garlic cloves, minced

1 Tbsp fresh ginger root, grated

2 tsp garam masala

¼ tsp red pepper flakes (adjust to taste)

2 medium sweet potatoes, peeled and chopped

1¾ cups fresh or frozen sour cherries

1 14-ounce (400 mL) can coconut milk

1 cup fresh spinach leaves

Kosher salt and ground black pepper, to taste

1. Place the olive oil in a large saucepan and heat over medium heat. Add the onion and cook until it is soft. Add the garlic, ginger root, garam masala, red pepper flakes, sweet potatoes, sour cherries, and coconut milk. Stir to combine.

2. Cook the curry for 20 minutes at a simmer, until the mixture thickens and the sweet potatoes become soft. Add the spinach and stir. Cook for another 5 minutes, until the spinach wilts. Take the curry off the heat. Add the salt and pepper, and serve.

Sour Cherry Glazed Chicken Wings

GF DF NF — *Makes 12 chicken wings to serve 2–4 people*

Saucy, sticky, and fruity—this is finger food at its finest. Do these up if you're having guests over to watch the game or to take along to a potluck. The wings become even more flavourful as leftovers, so go ahead and double the recipe!

1 Tbsp vegetable oil

12 chicken wings (tips removed)

1 Tbsp toasted sesame oil

½ tsp kosher salt

½ tsp ground black pepper

½ cup fresh sour cherries

½ cup ketchup

¼ cup apple cider vinegar

1 garlic clove, minced

1 Tbsp hot sauce (optional)

1. Preheat the oven to 350°F. Brush a 1.5-quart oven-safe baking dish with the vegetable oil.

2. Place the chicken wings, sesame oil, salt, and pepper in a large zippered plastic bag. Shake the bag until the chicken is coated with the oil mixture.

3. To make the glaze, place the sour cherries, ketchup, apple cider vinegar, garlic, and hot sauce (if using) in a medium bowl. Use an immersion or a regular blender to combine the ingredients.

4. Place the chicken wings in the baking dish in a single layer. Baste the wings with the cherry glaze.

5. Bake the chicken wings in the oven for 30 minutes, then turn them over in the pan. Brush them with more glaze. Bake the wings for another 30 minutes.

6. Remove the chicken wings from the oven and dig in!

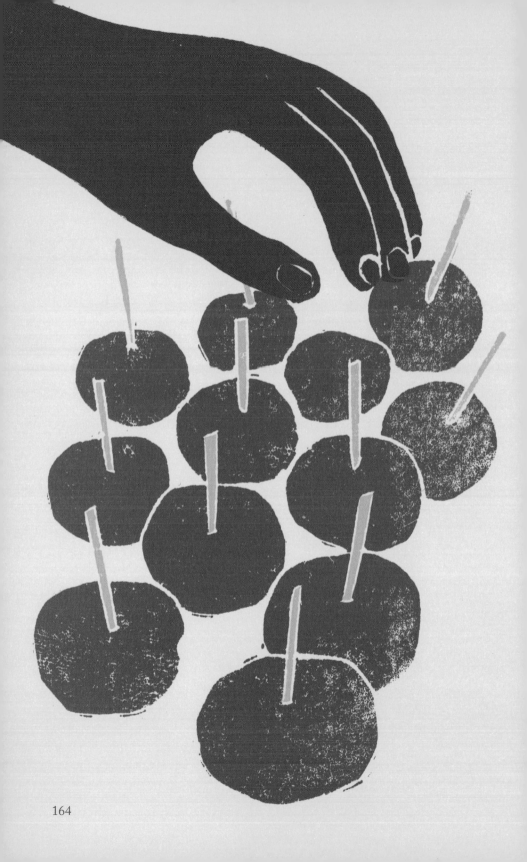

Lamb and Sour Cherry Meatballs

NF — *Makes 20 meatballs*

While this recipe is fantastic out of the gate, the leftovers are even more incredible, as the flavours will have had time to meld and improve. Don't be afraid to double this recipe and freeze the meatballs for later delectation. Slide a few in between two slices of thick, soft bread, add some really good mustard, and you have a serious sandwich!

1 Tbsp extra-virgin olive oil

1 small onion, minced

1 lb ground lamb

½ cup fresh or frozen sour cherries

1 egg

¼ cup chopped fresh parsley

2 Tbsp dried bread crumbs

1 tsp ground cumin

2 garlic cloves, minced

Kosher salt and ground black pepper, to taste

1 cup plain yogurt, for dipping

1. Preheat the oven to 350°F.

2. Place a piece of parchment paper on a baking sheet.

3. Combine all of the ingredients except for the yogurt in a large bowl until thoroughly mixed.

4. Roll the mixture into small balls, each approximately 1 inch in diameter. Place them on the prepared baking sheet.

5. Bake the meatballs in the oven for 30 minutes. Turn them over and bake them for another 10 minutes.

6. Remove the meatballs from the oven. Pierce each meatball with a toothpick and serve them with the yogurt for dipping.

Sour Cherry and Peanut Butter Bars

V — *Makes one 9- × 9-inch pan of bars*

These insanely delicious squares are like traditional PB&J bars, with one major update: because you are using fruit instead of sweetened preserves, the sugar content is lessened. It means there are *slightly* fewer calories, but you don't lose any of the scrumptious flavour, or the lunchbox-friendly portability.

½ cup unsalted butter, softened
½ cup granulated sugar
¼ cup creamy peanut butter
1 egg

1¾ cups all-purpose flour
½ cup unsalted peanuts, chopped finely
1½ cups fresh or frozen sour cherries

1. Preheat the oven to 350°F.

2. Place a sheet of parchment paper in a 9- × 9-inch baking pan.

3. Using a stand or hand-held mixer, in a large bowl mix the butter and sugar until light and fluffy. Add the peanut butter and egg and combine until the mixture is creamy. Add the flour and the peanuts. The mixture will now be crumbly.

4. Remove half of the mixture from the bowl and reserve. Press the remaining dough into the bottom of the baking pan so that it evenly covers the entire base of the pan. Spread the sour cherries on top in an even layer. Place chunks of the remaining dough on top of the sour cherries. There will be spaces in the dough where the cherries will show through. Gently press the dough chunks down so that they are slightly flattened.

5. Bake the bars in the oven for 45 to 50 minutes, until golden.

6. Completely cool the bars in the pan on a wire rack. Cut into squares and serve. Store the leftover bars in the refrigerator.

Puffed Rice Cereal Squares with Sour Cherries

NF V — *Makes about 16 squares*

Cereal isn't typically considered decadent, but these puffed rice cereal squares are an exception! The combination of dried sour cherries and butterscotch chips elevate a popular lunchbox add-in to party food, and you don't have to reveal just how easy it was to put them together. See pages 11 for step-by-step instructions to dehydrate the sour cherries you'll need in this recipe.

4 Tbsp unsalted butter, plus 1 tsp butter for greasing the pan
40 large marshmallows
4⅔ cups puffed rice cereal

1 cup dried sour cherries, chopped finely
½ cup butterscotch baking chips

1. Grease a 9- × 9-inch baking pan with 1 tsp butter.

2. In a large saucepan, melt the marshmallows and the 4 Tbsp butter over medium heat, stirring constantly. (Marshmallows can burn in an instant, so don't take your focus away from them!)

3. When the mixture is melted, remove the pan from the heat and stir in the puffed rice cereal, the sour cherries, and the butterscotch chips.

4. Press the cereal mixture into the prepared baking pan with a spatula. Use the spatula to pat down and level the mixture in the pan. Place the pan into the refrigerator for 2 hours to chill. Cut into squares and enjoy!

Sour Cherry Stovetop Cobbler

NF V — *Makes 4 dessert servings*

If you've ever made a traditional fruit cobbler, you know how simple it is to assemble the basic batter, spread it over fruit, and throw it in the oven for a half-hour or so. If you can believe it, this is even easier, as the dough is dropped into the hot fruit by the spoonful and it puffs up into fluffy dumplings. And did I mention you don't even need to turn on the oven?

FRUIT BASE

2 cups fresh or frozen sour cherries

½ cup water

¼ cup granulated sugar

1 tsp almond extract

DUMPLINGS

1 cup all-purpose flour

¼ cup sugar

1 tsp baking powder

½ cup low-fat milk

3 Tbsp unsalted butter, melted

1. Combine all the ingredients for the fruit base in a 6-quart Dutch oven. Heat to a simmer over medium heat. Allow the fruit to cook for 5 minutes.

2. To make the dumpling batter, mix together the flour, the sugar, and the baking powder in a medium bowl. Add the milk and the melted butter and stir just until combined.

3. Drop the batter by heaping tablespoonfuls into the hot fruit. (Each dumpling should be about 2 to 3 Tbsp.) Reduce the heat to medium-low. Cover the Dutch oven and allow the dumplings to cook on the stovetop for 15 minutes. Do not take the cover off during the cooking time or the steam will escape and the dumplings won't rise as much as they should.

Sour Cherry Pie

NF V — *Makes one 9-inch pie crust*

Pair this sweet pie filling with the flaky, tender pie crust on page 60. Feel free to swap out the sour cherries for saskatoons and make a saskatoon berry pie instead! Or make one of each. I'm just sayin'...

Pastry for a double crust pie (see page 60)
6 cups fresh sour cherries
⅓ cup granulated sugar
⅓ cup brown sugar
¼ cup cornstarch
1 Tbsp fresh lemon juice

¼ tsp ground cinnamon
¼ tsp ground cardamom
1 Tbsp unsalted butter
1 egg
1 Tbsp low-fat milk

1. Make your favourite double crust pastry or use my recipe on page 60. Shape dough into two discs, wrap in plastic wrap, and refrigerate until chilled.

2. Preheat the oven to 400°F.

3. Combine the sour cherries, both sugars, the cornstarch, the lemon juice, the cinnamon, and the cardamom in a large bowl.

4. On a well-floured work surface, roll out one of the discs in a 10-inch circle. Place in the bottom of a 9-inch pie pan. Spoon the filling into the bottom crust.

5. Cut the butter up into small pieces and dab them onto the pie filling.

6. Roll out the second pastry disc to a 10-inch circle. Cover the pie with the top crust and crimp the edges of the pastry together. Pierce the top crust with a fork in several places.

7. Make the egg wash by whisking the egg and the milk together in a small bowl. Use a pastry brush to brush the top of the pie.

8. Bake the pie for 20 minutes. Remove the pie from the oven and cover the edges with an aluminum foil shield (see page 61).

9. Turn the oven down to 375°F. Return the pie to the oven and bake for 30 minutes or until the crust is golden brown. Remove the pie from the oven and remove the foil edging. Allow the pie to thoroughly cool before serving.

Sour Cherry and Basil Rum Cocktail

GF DF NF V VG — *Makes approximately two 12-ounce drinks*

Enjoy summer in a glass! You may think that basil in a drink is wacky, but don't leave it out. It complements and enhances the sour cherry flavour and makes this particular cocktail dance. (Well, *someone* will be dancing if you drink enough of these!)

6 basil leaves
⅓ cup simple syrup (see page 73 for instructions)
Ice cubes
4 oz white rum
1 cup sour cherry juice (see page 15 for how to juice cherries)
1 cup lime-flavoured sparkling water

1. Combine the basil leaves and the simple syrup in a small saucepan. Bring to a boil over high heat. Remove the syrup from the heat and allow it to cool to room temperature. Refrigerate it for at least 1 hour before using.

2. Fill two tall glasses with ice. Place the basil simple syrup, the rum, and the sour cherry juice into a cocktail shaker and muddle. Divide the mixture between the two glasses and top with sparkling water.

    NOTE: To make this drink non-alcoholic, omit the rum.

Acknowledgements

A massive, heartfelt thank you to the incredibly talented, hard-working, and supportive publishing team at TouchWood Editions. I am so grateful to all of you for your encouragement and expertise, and deeply appreciate the amazing opportunity to make this idea a reality!

Such an honour and delight to have illustrators Tree Abraham and Meryl Hulse create all of the beautiful images for the book. Tree's design is absolutely gorgeous and unique. Thank you so much!

Everlasting gratitude and love to my mum and dad and my brother Derek. More of the same goes out to my husband, Rob, who made countless runs for flour, put up with me making jam or baking at 2 o'clock in the morning, and taste-tested all of the recipes in the book. A tough gig, but someone had to do it.

I've consulted many good resources over the years while gathering berry knowledge. A bibliography of my favourite berry-centric books and websites can be found on my website, floweryprose.com.

Index

Recipe names set in italics indicate ones in which the main ingredient it's listed under may be used as a substitute.

For more information, contact the publisher at:
TouchWood Editions
touchwoodeditions.com

The information in this book is true and complete to the best of the author's knowledge.
All recommendations are made without guarantee on the part of the author or the publisher.

Edited by Paula Marchese
Cover and interior design by Tree Abraham
Illustrations by Tree Abraham and Meryl Hulse

Cataloguing information available from Library and Archives Canada
ISBN 9781771513425 (softcover)
ISBN 9781771513432 (ebook)

TouchWood Editions acknowledges that the land on which we live and work is within
the traditional territories of the Lkwungen (Esquimalt and Songhees), Malahat, Pacheedaht,
Scia'new, T'sou-ke and WSÁNEĆ (Pauquachin, Tsartlip, Tsawout, Tseycum) peoples.

We acknowledge the financial support of the Government of Canada through the Canada
Book Fund, and the Province of British Columbia through the Book Publishing Tax Credit.

This book was printed using FSC-certified, acid-free papers, processed chlorine free,
and printed with soya-based inks.

Printed in China.

25 24 23 22 21 1 2 3 4 5